D0760155

Silver Creek
Idaho's Fly Fishing Paradise

To John,
May you always
dream of Streams

Dave

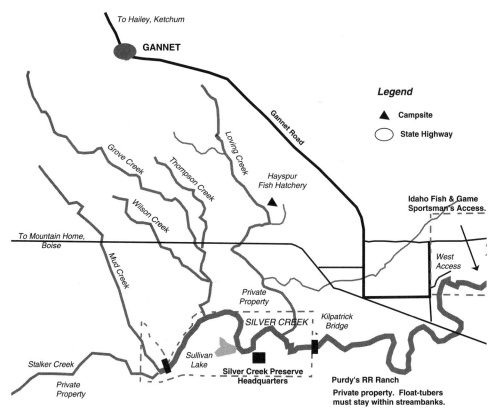

GANNET

Gannet Road

Grove Creek

Thompson Creek

Loving Creek

Wilson Creek

Hayspur
Fish Hatchery

Legend

▲ Campsite

◯ State Highway

**Idaho Fish & Game
Sportsman's Access.**

*West
Access*

To Mountain Home,
Boise

Mud Creek

*Private
Property*

SILVER CREEK

Kilpatrick
Bridge

Stalker Creek

*Sullivan
Lake*

**Silver Creek Preserve
Headquarters**

*Private
Property*

Purdy's RR Ranch

Private property. Float-tubers
must stay within streambanks.

Idaho

● Boise

Silver Creek

● Idaho Falls

● Twin Falls

● Pocatello

Silver Creek
and its tributaries

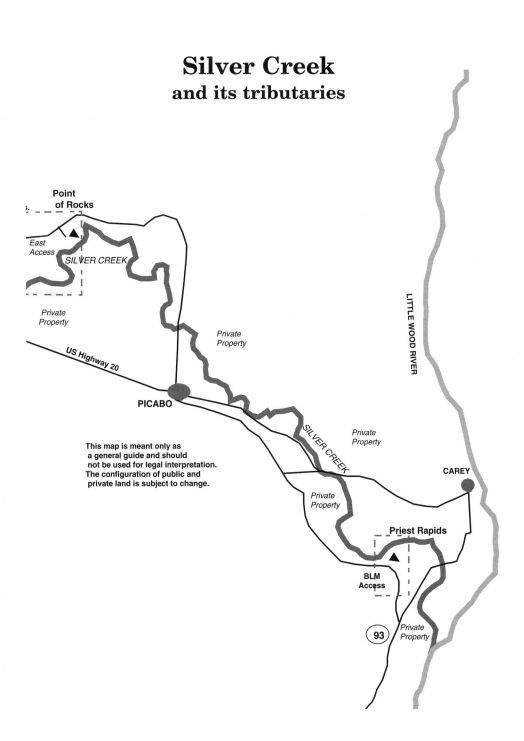

Point
of Rocks

East
Access

SILVER CREEK

Private
Property

US Highway 20

PICABO

This map is meant only as
a general guide and should
not be used for legal interpretation.
The configuration of public and
private land is subject to change.

Private
Property

Private
Property

SILVER CREEK

Private
Property

LITTLE WOOD RIVER

CAREY

Priest Rapids

Private
Property

BLM
Access

93

Private
Property

The
Nature
Conservancy®
OF IDAHO

State Office
P. O. Box 165
Sun Valley, ID 83353
TEL 208 726-3007
FAX 208 726-1258

North Idaho Program
East 1677 Miles Avenue
Hayden Lake, ID 83835
TEL 208 762-1307
FAX 208 762-1408

October 9, 1997

Dave Glasscock &
Dave Clark
P.O. Box 713
Picabo, ID 83348

Dear Dave and Dave,

I hope this reaches you on a beautiful fall day. We are nearing the end of another great season at Silver Creek Preserve. Over 12,000 people have enjoyed fishing, hiking, and canoeing at the preserve this year, and in spite of the increase in use, it is one of those unique places where the environment gets better every year. This is due to 20 years of care and restoration by the Conservancy, and the hard work of our neighbors who are farming and ranching the land in ways that respect the environment.

The Nature Conservancy began its work at Silver Creek in 1976. This was the first Nature Conservancy project in Idaho, and since that time we have gone on to protect over 200,000 acres of the state's most important natural lands. These include the spectacular Flat Ranch Preserve on the upper Henry's Fork of the Snake River, Thousand Springs Preserve near Hagerman, and Garden Creek Preserve in the heart of Hell's Canyon.

At Silver Creek, the Conservancy now owns 880 acres in the core preserve area, and through Conservation Easements we have protected another 8,000 acres and over 30 miles of Silver Creek and its tributaries from development and inappropriate land use. Much of what we do here is not readily apparent to our visitors, but it is critical to the long term health of Silver Creek. Stewardship activities at the preserve include visitor use management, trail maintenance, and merchandise sales. We work with our neighbors to keep livestock and crop production from damaging the streamside habitat, we purchase additional land and monitor conservation easements, and we host fundraising events which raise money to support our operations.

Our annual expenses exceed $120,000, and we rely entirely on donations to accomplish our work. Historically we have not required a fee for fishing on the preserve, and we hope to keep it that way. But we will only be able to do this if our visitors donate at least $5 per visit or become a member of The Nature Conservancy for $25 per year (or a Friend of Silver Creek for $100 per year). What I hope people understand is that we are in this together, and because The Nature Conservancy is a private, non-profit organization, the preserve's future depends on supporters at all levels.

Thanks for all that you have done to help us keep Silver Creek Preserve such a special place. Please call me any time if you have questions or thoughts about the Conservancy's work.

Best Wishes,

Paul Todd
Silver Creek Area Manager

Silver Creek Preserve
P. O. Box 624
Picabo, ID 83348
TEL 208 788-2203

Upper Henry's Fork Project
HC 66, Box 227
Island Park, ID 83429
TEL 208 558-9626
FAX 208 558-9622

Thousand Springs Preserve
1205 Thousand Springs Grade
Wendell, ID 83355
TEL 208 536-6797

Garden Creek Preserve
Snake River Route
Lewiston, ID 83501
TEL 208 243-4055

Silver Creek
Idaho's Fly Fishing Paradise

David Clark and David Glasscock

The CAXTON PRINTERS, Ltd.
Caldwell, Idaho
1997

Library of Congress Cataloging-in-Publication Data

Clark, Dave (David R.)
  Silver Creek: Idaho's Fly Fishing Paradise / Dave Clark, Dave
Glasscock.
  p. cm.
  Includes bibliographical references (p.   ) and index.
  ISBN 0-87004-382-X
  1. Fly Fishing – Idaho – Silver Creek (Blaine County) 2. Silver
Creek (Blaine County, Idaho) I. Glasscock, Dave, 1955- .
  II. Title.
  SH487.C58   1997
  799.1'757'0979632--dc21   97-33288
                                                          CIP

Lithographed and bound in the United States of America by
The Caxton Printers, Ltd.
Caldwell, Idaho
162405

Acknowledgements

Fly fishing is a solitary sport, but its often more fun when you share your experiences with a companion. Writing is also a solitary pursuit made more enjoyable when good people are willing to share your triumphs and frustrations.

We would like to thank a number of people who assisted us in one way or the other with the creation of this book. Special thanks to Wayne Cornell, our editor at The Caxton Printers, Ltd. It was his faith in us and his incredible talent that made the book possible.

We also are indebted to Dr. Mel Kuntz. A geologist by profession, but a fly fisherman at heart, Mel was both a diligent and enlightening editor.

Our thanks to the Silver Creek Preserve and Nature Conservancy Staff – Guy Bonnivier, Paul Todd, Mud Watters, Cindy and Lou Lunte, and so many others who shared their knowledge with us and whose dedication has made Silver Creek one of the greatest streams in the world. We also gained inspiration from Frank Gift, who was a friend to everyone who came to fish Silver Creek and was called by his maker in the middle of a backcast to a Silver Creek brown.

Special acknowledgement is also due to the body of scientific knowledge Dr. Jack Griffin and his associates at Idaho State University have amassed to allow us to better understand the complexities of these unique waters. For their very special expertise and willingness to share it, we owe C. E. Brockway, hydrologist with the University of Idaho, and Dr. Dwight Schmidt, geologist with the U.S. Geologic Survey, our gratitude. We are also greatful to Jim Gabettas for sharing his indepth understanding of fish and fly fishing in Idaho

Our appreciation to Ed Berg from Sunnyvale, California who, as a demonstration fly tier at the Fly Fishers International Conclave at Lewiston, Montana, gave us a couple of simple tips that greatly improved the design of our Poly Parachute fly.

A very loving thanks to Lorraine and Ginny. There are some wives who might complain when their husbands went fishing seven days a week, but not these two.

And finally, our best to everyone who fishes Silver Creek, releases its treasures unharmed, and goes away realizing they owe something to the stream and earth that has refreshed their spiritual being.

Contents

Maps, Illustrations and Photos

– – –

Color Photos

Introduction

My earliest recollection of Silver Creek is the water's calm surface temporarily etched with the rings caused by dozens of rising trout. The spreading circles mesmerized me because, like a kid receiving brightly wrapped presents at Christmas, I knew each one contained a wonderful surprise.

For the trout, the rise is only an instinctual response – the quick whip of the tail, the ability to accurately calculate the movement of a target, and the robot-like opening and closing of the jaws. Being successful means life. Failure is death. At Silver Creek, it is easy to be successful.

For the insects, the rise is nothing but a funeral. But for every hundred insects that end up in the belly of a fish, one or two succeed in reproducing. This has proven to be enough.

For the biologist, the rise signals the end of a long progression of a predictable, but none-the-less, incredible sequence of events where the spark of life is combined with water, chemicals, and the energy of the sun to create a hatch of insects – a collective mass of protein quickly swallowed by hungry trout. The chain of events is a simple predatory incident that occurs thousands of times today, and will occur thousands of times tomorrow.

For the angler, the rise provokes a yet undefined reaction. Some call the mini-jolt to our senses caused by the sight of a rising trout a response to the hunter instincts of our past. But this explanation is too simple. Riseforms trigger a host of emotions – excitement, anticipation, amazement, longing, elation, exhilaration – each quite capable of causing an angler to fish for hours, for days, or for a lifetime. Rises cast a spell that no one, especially the angler, can understand.

The rise is that rare example of perfection – perfect perception, perfect reflexes, and perfect timing. To watch the rise of a feeding fish is to observe an exquisite display of accuracy and precision honed by eons of selection. Our ability to fool an occasional trout into taking a phony fly allows us to become a part of this incredible moment, and, for a brief instant, to be almost perfect ourselves. Our addiction to this feeling is why we fish.

This book is dedicated to the magic of the rise, hatching insects, bulging trout, and to a stream that conceived and nurtures them – Silver Creek.

* * *

Because we agreed on nearly everything in the book and because we have the misfortune of both having the same first name, we felt that it would be easiest to just refer to ourselves as "I." Where we did have different opinions we simply stated both viewpoints.

Dave Clark and David Glasscock
July 4, 1997, Arco and Picabo, Idaho

1
The Heart of Idaho

At one time, I fished Silver Creek with a near obsession. I can remember fishing the stream seven days a week. I can recall standing in the same spot for five hours, both feet tingling from a lack of blood flow, casting to one rising fish after another. And, I think it was me, who one July day, began by imitating Tricos at 6 A.M. and successively fished imitations of blue-winged-olives, Callibaetis, pale morning duns, damsels, hoppers, small, brown caddis and, after dark, leaches. On that day I fished Silver Creek for nearly eighteen straight hours – leaving only when I zinged a fly into the back of my hand and couldn't see well enough to remove it.

Today, many years later, my obsession is different. I still fish, but now I occasionally spend my time sitting on the stream bank watching birds appropriately called flycatchers snatching caddisflies bobbing up and down just over the water's surface. Or I find myself laying on my belly in the early calm just after dawn attempting to photograph the wild iris before the morning breeze arrives to jiggle the flower out of focus. And occasionally, I just wander around, looking for nothing other than something I have never experienced before. Silver Creek never disappoints me.

The Center of Idaho

If you open an Idaho road map and point to the exact center of state, your finger will be located only slightly north of Silver Creek. By highway, Silver Creek is 135 miles west of

Contemplating the hatch.

Boise, Idaho's capital and its largest city (in Idaho it only takes 150,000 citizens to acquire this distinction). The stream is also 120 miles east of Idaho Falls, the gateway to Yellowstone National Park, sixty miles north of the state's bread basket, Twin Falls, and thirty-five miles south of Sun Valley, the first destination ski resort in the United States and Idaho's sole island of liberalism.

For the naturalist, Silver Creek symbolizes the wild heart of Idaho. It is a place where you can stumble over a mule deer asleep in the shade of a sagebrush, smell the sweet fragrance of a wild rose blossom, or watch a rough-legged hawk drop out of the sky to capture a deer mouse. This is the side of Silver Creek that turns the heads of even the most dedicated fishing addicts and convinces them there are a few other sights just as incredible as a trout rising to a fly.

To the geologist, Silver Creek is also the heartland or focal point where powerful geologic forces once met. Sandwiched between the Pioneer, Smoky and Boulder Mountains to the north and the Snake River Plain to the south, Silver Creek was created where a dam of lava rock trapped a slurry of sand, pebbles and boulders scraped from the Earth's face by glacial scalpels. Silver Creek exists where the mountains and lava now touch.

And finally, for anglers Silver Creek is the heart of the sport of fly fishing for trout in Idaho. Most anglers try Idaho's other rivers – the Henry's Fork, Big Lost, South Fork of the Snake, or the Big Wood – before taking on the challenge of Silver Creek. But Silver Creek's reputation beckons and once anglers tie into one of the stream's rambunctious rainbows or brutish browns, they often lose their own hearts to this stream.

Of Fire and Ice

Like a child who looks like neither of its parents, the Silver Creek which seeps out of the ground and placidly meanders across grassy pastures and fields of alfalfa, bears little resemblance to the awesome powers that created it. No mild-mannered ancestors here, Silver Creek is the result of a union of molten lava and frozen ice. To understand Silver Creek's strange family tree, it's necessary to go far back into the geologic past.

The basement rock that makes up the foundation of southern Idaho formed about one billion of years ago when immense oceans covered much of the Earth. During this aquatic period, anything – gravel, soil or dead animals – that found its way into these large bodies of water was eventually deposited as part of a blanket of ooze on the sea floor.

These layers of organic and inorganic materials became what geologist refer to as "sedimentary" rock and their composition depended on their varied ingredients. Waves that crashed onto the beach churned up sand that was compressed into hundred- foot bands of sandstone. When rushing rivers slowed, they dumped clay silt, and gravel pebbles on top of each other to form parallel layers of shale and conglomerate. And when the trillions of marine invertebrates died, their shells drifted down to the ocean floor and were altered and compacted into limestone. Eventually, the seas subsided and all that remained behind were the pancake-like stacks of sedimentary rock; a stone frosting that covered much of Idaho and North America.

For hundreds of millions of years following the buildup of

sedimentary rock, a virtual smorgasbord of catastrophic events took place in Idaho. In discussing these phenomenon, geologists use such jargon as "metamorphosed, intrusions, plutons, orogeny and porphyritic." For the non-scientist, these terms simply mean the landscape went through one severe convulsion after the other. And during these spasms, the rock that now makes up the mountains of south-central Idaho was folded, thrust upward, fractured, cooked, ruptured, and blasted into the atmosphere. And then, as soon as the rocky spires tectonic forces had worked so hard to erect were in place, the more persistent power of gravity began working to bring them down.

Gradually, the scouring action of the wind, rain and glacial ice carved these layers of rock, volcanic ash and isolated pockets of speckled granite into the Boulder, Pioneer, and other mountain ranges. The erosional scars – the canyons, washes, and gullies – directed thousands of rivulets of water into what was to become the Big Wood River. For millions of years, the Big Wood River carried the runoff from the winter's snowpack and summer's thunderstorms out of the mountains and across the flatlands below. Then, with the awakening of the volcanoes of the Snake River Plain, the river's course was altered.

The Snake River Plain is a broad, flat, arc of lava that spans southern Idaho from border to border. Geologists believe the plain was created as the North American continent moved over a stationary hot spot – a geologic blowtorch beneath the crust capable of melting the overlying rock. As the resulting flux of molten crust surged upward, the Earth's surface bulged, cracked and finally exploded. Colossal eruptions blasted huge holes as much as ten miles in diameter into the Earth's crust at many places along the entire length of the Snake River Plain. These large craters are known as calderas. In comparison, if the eruption of Mount St. Helen's was the plink of a 22-caliber rimfire, then these detonations were the blast of a Tomahawk missile.

As the ever moving North American continent slid over the hot spot at a rate of about two inches per year – about the same speed as your fingernail grows – the focal point of the eruptions constantly changed. Each subsequent eruption became part of a volcanic track of successively younger calderas strung out in a

A lava flow similar to the one that dammed the Big Wood River.

line from west to east. The oldest eruptions occurred more than sixteen million years ago near the Idaho-Oregon border. Today, the hot spot that once kept the central Idaho landscape in continual (geologically speaking) upheaval is keeping the geysers of Yellowstone National Park boiling and threatens to turn the entire area into a parking lot paved in hot ash sometime in the distant future. The most recent activity in Yellowstone occurred 600,000 years ago and, according to the experts, should erupt again within the next 100,000 years.

But even though the hot spot is now located under Yellowstone, residual heat keeps the Snake River Plain fuming with volcanic activity. Although it has been nearly five million years since the hot spot was in the vicinity of Silver Creek, volcanic eruptions blanketed the area with hot cinders and liquefied rock much more recently. Only thirty miles away at Craters of the Moon National Monument, lava has erupted within the last 2,000 years. Like charcoal in a barbecue, it takes a long time for the fire in the Earth's crust to cool.

When compared to the caldera forming eruptions, this second stage of volcanic activity on the Snake River Plain consisted of rather docile discharges of a fluid, black lava known as basalt. These eruptions were similar to the spurting, splashing,

surging lava flows that periodically pour out of volcanoes in
Hawaii where, instead of blasting fragments of lava into the
stratosphere, most of the basaltic lava simply wells to the surface and gently flows away from open vents or cracks.

It was just such a lava flow that oozed out of a vent near the
headwaters of present day Silver Creek, crossed the Big Wood

River, and, damming
it, created a large
lake. Later, as the Big
Wood River entered
the lake and slowed,
the sediments it held
in suspension were
dumped, piling up on
the lake bottom.

The rate of depo-
sition of this
lake-floor debris

Big Wood River seeps underground.   increased dramatically with the onset of the ice age. As the world's climate cooled,
glaciers formed in the mountains of central Idaho. These ice
masses etched and scraped the face of the mountains, breaking
off and transporting enormous amounts of material. Year after
year, like litter along the side of a highway, fragmented stone
accumulated at the base of these tall peaks.

Then, as the Earth warmed once more, the glaciers and
snow fields started to melt. Rivers with runoff equal to four
times the maximum flows of today, scooped up the rock particles
stockpiled at the base of mountain slopes and swept them away.
The rushing water carried untold tons of sand, pebbles and
small boulders into the Big Wood River. Once again, this material came to rest at the lake as the stream completed its descent
and lost its energy. As a result, large amounts of marble-, golf
ball-, and baseball-sized gravel was added to the lake bottom.

This accumulation of sediment rapidly filled the lake basin
and the channel of the Big Wood River gradually reappeared as
the river cut through the conglomeration of material. As the
years went by, periodic volcanic eruptions led to the continued
formation of lakes in the same general location along with the

subsequent alteration of the Big Wood River's course. Sometimes the river ran through the Picabo area, sometimes it followed its present course towards the southwest.

Today, when the river reaches the old lake-site at the mouth of the Big Wood Canyon, the deposits of sand, pea-gravel, and river-polished stones act like a sponge to soak up much of the passing water. It is this water that eventually gave birth to Silver Creek.

Outpouring of Water

The source of the water that spawns Silver Creek starts with the tiny rivulets that drain the large snow fields high in the watershed of the Smoky, Boulder and Pioneer Mountains. As small threads of water gather together, they collectively form the tributaries of the Big Wood River. Early residents named some of these water courses for the people who discovered them or, at least, were judged remarkable enough to deserve lasting recognition. Hence Murdock, Adams, Baker, Croy and Quigley Creeks were named for local characters. Other streams were named by those more enchanted by the local wildlife than people. Today, these are still known as Owl, Eagle, Deer and Fox Creeks. And finally, a few streams – Slaughterhouse, Indian, Corral and Greenhorn Creek – were christened for reasons known only to early explorers and settlers.

Along a common fifty-mile long corridor, all of these creeks ultimately link up to form the Big Wood River. The remote headwaters of the Big Wood are located on the steep sides of a dozen mountain peaks that range from 9,000 to 12,000 feet in elevation. On these barren slopes of talus, nothing grows except a few scattered, stunted trees and the occasional wildflower. Flowing out of snowfields that cover these lofty crests for most of the year, tributaries of the Big Wood River quickly descend through ravines lined with the spruce and fir of the Sawtooth National Forest. The drop in elevation is constant until the topography flattens near the town of Ketchum. Here, the Big Wood River winds between the million dollar homes – streamside property expensive even for a resort community – until it exits its canyon passageway at the town of Bellevue.

After reaching the bottomlands, most of the water in the

Big Wood River continues a short journey to the impoundment known as Magic Reservoir. Just prior to flowing into the reservoir, however, the stream passes over the same glacially deposited sediment – alluvium – that is being mined by several sand and gravel suppliers. Here, a large amount of water seeps into the ground only to resurface ten miles away as the springs that form the tributaries of Silver Creek.

During the summer months, however, so much of the water in the Big Wood is diverted into irrigation canals near Bellevue that the river virtually "dries" up. Fortunately, water carried to the east in ditches now becomes the primary source of recharge for the springs that form Silver Creek.

The Birth of Silver Creek

Underground, water from the Wood River forms a southerly flowing aquifer that percolates through layers of sandstone, siltstone and limestone – the bottoms of those ancient oceans – and the sediments deposited in glacial times. Then, as the moving water comes into contact with the solid, dense, impermeable rock of the Picabo Hills, its flow is suddenly blocked. Unable to continue its journey, the water is forced to the surface where it bubbles out as springs. The flow from more than a dozen of these springs ultimately creates Stalker, Grove, Loving and several smaller creeks. It is where these streams join that Silver Creek is born.

Today, as water in the aquifer moves through underground strata and sediments, it absorbs calcium carbonate from limestones, phosphates from phosphatic sediments, and other minerals and chemicals that are crucial in supporting a diverse, healthy aquatic ecosystem. Beneath the surface, the subterranean rocks and sediments warms or cools the water in the aquifer to a temperature that is always, summer or winter, at or near fifty-two degrees. And, having flowed through filters of lava, sand and gravel, any impurities or harmful toxins present in the water of the Big Wood River have been removed. The final result is Silver Creek – a stream containing water like few others.

Silver Creek.

Silver Creek

Reborn, the new stream no longer resembles its parent river, the Big Wood. No more rolling ripples, splashing swirls or churning rapids. Silver Creek is canal-like slow and seemingly takes forever to meander through The Nature Conservancy's Silver Creek Preserve, or as most call it "The Conservancy." The stream then winds through a private ranch and then into an Idaho Department of Fish and Game sportsman's access area at Point of Rocks (named for the rocky outcroppings at the site). The stream then saunters past the farms and ranches surrounding the tiny agricultural community of Picabo.

Silver Creek crosses Highway 20 twice as it moves to the north and then, to the south. After crossing the highway for the second time just east of Picabo, the creek picks up speed and takes a more direct route as it heads into a small lava canyon on land managed by the Bureau of Land Management. This area is known as Priest Rapids. In this small volcanic gorge, water bounces over and around boulders creating depressions that could pass for pools. As the stream leaves BLM land, it again enters private property and reverts to its slow moving

Little Wood River

character. Four miles south, Silver Creek pours into the Little Wood River flowing out of the mountains north of Carey, Idaho. "Flowing out" might be putting it a bit strongly. Except during spring runoff, farmers divert nearly all of the water in the Little Wood River to irrigate their fields.

Regardless of what stream supplies the water, the river below this junction is named the Little Wood and flows along the edge of the Snake River Plain and somehow keeps from disappearing into the porous lava as do other streams such as the Big Lost River which sinks below the surface fifty miles to the east. Depending on how the river has cut into the black rock, the Little Wood is a stream with every type of water: swift, shooting chutes, pulsating pocket water, and deep, dark pools where you can never see the bottom.

As the golden eagle flies, Silver Creek is fifteen miles from start to finish. When the length of its smaller, headwater tributaries and the river's natural meandering are considered the length of this aquatic system nearly doubles. From its headwaters to its confluence with the Little Wood River, Silver Creek loses 290 feet in elevation and, in the summer, is gradually warmed by twenty degrees or more. It crosses through two miles of the Silver Creek Preserve, another two miles within a Sportsman's Access, one mile of BLM land, and more than ten miles of private property.

A snowflake that lands at the top of the 12,009 foot high Hyndman Peak in the Pioneer Mountains has the potential to melt and flow all the way to the Pacific Ocean. But its chances of making it to the sea are remote; it is much more likely that the water molecules of the original snowflake will be absorbed by the roots of a willow, drunk by a mule deer, or diverted into a field by a farmer. Everything that lives along the length of Silver Creek depends on the stream's water for both life and pleasure.

2
From Sage to Shining Sage

I never appreciated sagebrush country until I started hunting sage grouse. For me, grouse hunting in southern Idaho is as mindless a pursuit as can be found anywhere. Every hunt is the same; walk through a sea of pale green shrubs that force you to take one step forward, one step to the side, one step forward, one step to the side. After a couple of hours in the field, this repetitive movement has a hypnotic effect. When this dull routine was coupled with a landscape void of any identifiable features — no hills, no gullies, no trees – I begin to wonder if I had been hunting the same plot over and over.

Although I'm sure there are outdoor writers who could write an entire book on "How to Hunt Sage Grouse," I've boiled it down to the simplest of tactics. First, meander around aimlessly until a bird jumps up. Then, while your mind is still engaged in the anticipation of your next sidestep, respond to the sudden flush of a grouse with reflexes so slow the bird gets a good five seconds to clear out. Shoot. Miss.

After using this jump and miss strategy on several hunting trips, I decided I could only improve by concentrating on the world within the range of my shotgun. This turned out to be difficult until I started to scrutinize the ground in front of me for anything that wasn't sagebrush. I was amazed at what I saw.

I found wildflowers – deep red Indian paintbrush, beautifully sculptured, porcelain-white sego lilies and the horn-shaped, blue larkspur – sprinkled among the shrubs. I watched dusky-colored sage sparrows, melodious yellow-striped meadowlarks and ground- nesting mourning doves flutter in and out of the sage. And, on rare occasions, I would glimpse a coyote I had spooked off a deer carcass – some hunter's mistake.

Once, when scrambling downhill through a stand of sage so dense I couldn't see my feet, I had my first, up-close contact with a badger. At least I think it was a badger. I can't imagine anything else that would hiss and spit like this unseen animal did.

In the end, did my new approach improve my hunting ability? Well, no. In fact, this technique didn't work as well because I would become so engrossed in the sage world I was discovering, the grouse would now get a ten second head start. I continue to hunt, but now the Zen of sage grouse hunting has more to do with experiencing this fascinating habitat than knocking down a bird.

Sage Desert

The sagebrush country that surrounds Silver Creek is a high, cold desert characterized by limited moisture, extreme temperatures and persistent winds. The annual average precipitation is a measly fifteen inches. Sitting in the rain shadow of the Cascade and Sierra mountain ranges of Washington, Oregon, and California, rainfall here is as scarce as an Idahoan wearing a tie.

During the summer, when an occasional surge of moisture-laden air invades the Great Basin (the immense bowl of land between the Pacific coastal mountains and the Rocky Mountains), thunderstorms develop as thermals lift moisture laden air. Rain from these storms may be heavy at times, but downpours capable of making mud are rare. The average rainfall during July and August is less than one inch per month.

In southern Idaho, most precipitation falls as snow in the winter. The heaviest snowfall occurs when the jet stream takes a long run over the Pacific Ocean off the coast of California and then heads inland. When this warm, moist air collides with the cold cell that sits over Idaho for most of the winter, snow flies. Three feet of snow at Donner Pass in California's Sierra-Nevada Mountains usually means at least a foot of new snowpack on the top of the mountains that surround Sun Valley. But although a couple of feet of snow can accumulate along the banks of Silver Creek or on the sagebrush lowlands by March, most of the water from the melting snow evaporates or runs off by the time the growing season arrives.

Sagebrush: One of nature's most adaptable plants.

Daily temperatures in southern Idaho have an Arctic/Sahara flavor to them. In the winter, daytime high temperatures are in the twenties and nighttime temperatures below zero are common. When the jet stream heads into Canada then turns south into Idaho, temperatures below minus forty degrees cause trees to snap from the cold.

In the summer, temperatures sizzle above ninety degrees during hot spells. And although the days may be quite warm, nighttime temperatures are always cool. This occurs because the light-colored soil and pale plants reflect away much of the sun's solar radiation and prevent heat from being absorbed during the day. Then at night, the small amount of heat retained in the sparse plant growth and the loose, dry soil quickly dissipates. A swing of more than thirty degrees between day and nighttime temperatures is common during the summer.

Here, in the land where lip balm could be sold by the gallon, dry, southwesterly winds blow in both summer and winter and rob the land, plants and animals of life-giving water. The wind is so persistent Idaho fly fishermen wear out five windbusting, weight-forward fly lines for every dainty doubletapered one they replace. Here, plants, animals and humans, are sun-bleached and parched or frost-bitten and numb from prolonged exposure to the climate. Fortunately for all of these organisms, none of them "just stand there and take it."

In southern Idaho, as well as in the entire Great Basin, the plant best adapted to these harsh conditions is the sagebrush.

The sagebrush is the climax vegetation in this area. That is, these are the plants that dominate the landscape and are best suited to growing in this environment.

Sage's amazing ability to conquer all adversity is shown by the fact that the shrub covers thousands of square miles of rangeland in the west. Hated by ranchers because cattle find it unpalatable, sage has been set on fire, soaked in herbicide, scraped away by road graders, and, with a chain suspended between two D-10 caterpillar tractors, jerked up by its roots. Through all of this, the sagebrush persists – a miracle of a plant that has survived everyone's wrath since the days of the pioneer.

The sagebrush is successful because it has adapted well to ultra-dry conditions. This plant is an engineering masterpiece – the ultimate in dryland vegetation. The sage's most important adaptation is its massive, three-tiered root system. Growing just below the surface, the sage has a bundle of fibrous roots that drink up any water as soon as it hits the ground. Below these, a second set of roots reach two feet underground to take advantage of snowmelt or heavy rain that seeps into this zone. Finally, extending as much as ten feet beneath the surface is a tap root that can take advantage of deep water. Collectively, the root mass of the sagebrush is so large that if a crane were used to pull an old sagebrush plant out of the ground, it would create a hole in which you could bury my fourteen-year-old Chevy pickup truck – an idea with certain appeal.

Sagebrush adaptations continue. The sagebrush is capable of growing leaves of different sizes; large leaves in the cool spring and small leaves in the hot summer. Large leaves provide for a burst of photosynthetic production early in the year when growing conditions are optimal. Diminutive leaves expose a minimum of surface area to the drying effects of the sun and wind. The conversion to smaller leaves in the summer conserves water as the temperature rises and soil moisture disappears.

A close inspection of the leaves of the sage reveals they are covered with light-colored hairs. These seemingly insignificant filaments reflect sunlight away from the leaf, prevent the wind from blowing directly across the surface of the leaf, and trap a layer of air on the surface of the leaf that holds in humidity.

Each of these characteristics helps to keep the surface of the leaves cool and reduce evaporation.

Each leaf is also covered with a pungent oil that gives sage its distinctive aroma. A coating of these volatile substances serves as a barrier to keep moisture from escaping.

Finally, even when the leaves of sagebrush die and fall away, they continue to help the plant. As the cast-off foliage breaks down, it releases chemicals into the soil that inhibit the growth of competing plants. With all of these adaptations and an ability for each plant to produce more than one million seeds, it's easy to understand why sagebrush is the most common shrub in North America.

Wild Onion

Although sagebrush dominates the ecosystem, there are still many niches for other plants. Grasses such as fescue and wheatgrass sprout and grow in the pockets of open space between the sage. These grasses have extremely shallow root systems that act as a blotter to absorb surface water before it is soaked up by the sage. Buckwheat and balsamroot are two herbaceous perennials that also do well in the sage desert because, for their size, they have immense root systems.

Wildflowers such as the wild onion and Indian paintbrush also do well intermixed with the sage. Every plant, however, must have some special adaptation – the onion has a water storing bulb, the paintbrush can grow as a parasite attaching itself to the roots of other plants – to give it the edge it needs to survive in this land of extremes.

Because of the lack of resources – water and soil – and the severe climate, the variety of plants in what is called the "cold desert" is limited and few species occur in large numbers. These same factors affect the animal community that relies on these plants for nourishment and protective cover.

Most of the smaller mammals of sagebrush country have

two traits in common: they eat plants and live underground for much of their lives. The yellow- bellied marmot is commonly seen in the early spring as it emerges from its winter hibernation. The marmot fattens itself on early blooming herbs and forbs and then, when the hot temperatures of summer arrive, returns to its underground shelter to aestivate – a type of dormancy where metabolism, heart rate and respiration are greatly slowed. Like wealthy New Yorkers who spend the hot summer at their New England beach house and the winter in a resort in the Bahamas, the marmot does whatever it takes to be comfortable and may spend less than four months each year above ground.

Other animals, like the badger and the Columbian ground squirrel, dig burrows for protection from the winter cold or summer heat. The Nuttall's cottontail rabbit, the pygmy rabbit, and the coyote all seek out unoccupied burrows or crevices in rocky cliffs as safe havens to raise their young.

The large mammals like the mule deer can't go underground when it is hot, so they seek whatever shade is available. On those sweaty afternoons of summer, I have seen these animals lying in the shade of a road cut to stay cool. On a scorcher of a day, even a truck driving down the road won't get the deer up until they are nearly run over.

In mid-summer, mule deer stay cool by being active only at night and keeping their movements to a minimum during the daytime heat. In early summer, deer can survive on the moisture contained in the vegetation they eat. But as the hot sun and wind dehydrates the plants, deer must find another water source. In the sagebrush desert, this may mean traveling long distances to reach streams like Silver Creek.

With the arrival of winter's cold, small mammals like the deer mouse are in danger of freezing to death if they don't find shelter. Often smaller mammals pass the winter inside a burrow in the ground or in a snow bank. Here they are protected because temperatures where the snow pack meets the ground remain constant at thirty-two degrees, regardless of the air temperature.

Large mammals retain heat better than the smaller animals because proportionately, much less of the surface of their

Mule deer on alert.

body is exposed to heat-robbing elements. Most of the larger animals modify their behavior in order to survive the winter. Well before the depth of the snowpack reaches their bellies, deer migrate to more hospitable areas – southern exposures where the sun melts and the wind blasts the snow off the ground, where solar radiation is at a maximum and forage such as mountain mahogany, bitterbrush or sagebrush is exposed.

The melting of the snow that covers the sage flatlands coincides with the arrival of many species of birds. The mourning dove and horned lark nest on the ground between the sage. Other birds, like the sage sparrow, Brewer's blackbird, and sage thrasher nest in the sage's foliage. Many of these birds spend the summer near Silver Creek, but migrate south in autumn. However, birds such as the northern harrier, a hawk easily distinguished by its prominent white rump, stay in the area as long as prey is available. Harriers raise their young on the flats (nesting on the ground) that surround Silver Creek and frequently "dive bomb" a fisherman who gets too close to their nest. Once in the attack mode, these birds have a tendency to overdo it. In order to protect myself, I admit that I have flicked my fly rod at more than one of these overzealous birds.

Other year-round residents include the raven, magpie, and sage grouse. As a group, these are some of the toughest birds found anywhere. To survive sub-zero temperatures and blasting wind, these birds must be hardened to their winter environment. The magpies and ravens survive by being smart, aggressive, and by eating anything they can get their bills around. Magpies are masters at finding the carcasses of dead animals. It is rare that a hunter can return to a gut pile left after dressing out an elk or deer without finding a magpie feast. Ravens have been known to follow coyotes in hopes that the animal will be successful in catching prey. When the coyotes have eaten their fill, the ravens dine on the leftovers.

Ravens and magpies have also learned that our highways are virtual cafeterias of squashed rabbits and splattered deer. Motorists often see this bird on the top of a road sign while anxiously waiting for the next accident.

You may find sagebrush without sage grouse, but you will never find a sage grouse without sagebrush growing nearby. The sage grouse depends on the this plant for shelter, nesting sites, and food. During the summer, this bird augments its diet of young plant shoots and insects with the leaves of sagebrush. In the winter, the grouse's survival totally depends on a diet of the sagebrush. Fortunately for the sage grouse, sage is an evergreen and remains a reliable source of food throughout the winter. To confirm the fact that the sage grouse literally has sage in its blood, a person needs only to try cooking up an old cock sage grouse – the aroma tells it all.

Reptiles are well represented in the sagebrush. The most common are the short-horned lizard – the "horny toad" – and the western skink. If you come across what you believe to be the world's largest earthworm, it is undoubtedly a snake known as the rubber boa. The snake Silver Creek visitors are most concerned about running into is the western rattlesnake – the snake with the diamondback pattern on its scales.

In all the years I have been wandering the banks of Silver Creek, I can only remember one encounter with one of these serpents. It was late evening, and I was walking down the trail that skirts the Lower Slough. Suddenly, a two-foot-long rattler appeared in the middle of the trail. With a girth larger than a baseball bat, this pudgy individual wouldn't do much to verify the rumor that a rattlesnake can strike a distance equal to one-third its length. This roly-poly snake would be lucky to be able strike a distance equal to one-third of its width! The uneventful experience ended as I watched the reptile slowly slither – no chug – off the trail, a living testimonial to the abundance of small mammals at Silver Creek. Regardless of my limited experience with rattlesnakes, other people report frequently seeing snakes in the vicinity of Silver Creek. Watch out for them. You may find a mean, skinny one.

I haven't yet mentioned insects because my interest in them is directly related to how important they are to the trout. But as with many people, when I discount "bugs," I am only showing my ignorance. Just what an important role the insects play in a ecosystem was recently demonstrated to me by an entomologist friend of mine. To justify his powerful reverence for insects, he pointed out

Yellow-Headed Blackbird

that while most people would pick the mule deer as the organism having the most significant impact on the sage ecosystem, millions of ants have a collective appetite that would put a deer to shame. I don't yet have the expertise to discuss all of the insects found near Silver Creek, but I now find my curiosity aroused every time I see a new bug – even if isn't found floating in the water.

Many people perceive sagebrush country to be a monotonous, wasteland. It's too bad they never stop their car, get out, and take a few steps into this miniature forest. After a closeup view of what is a fantastic natural community, they might understand why sageland doesn't have to be grazed, plowed or developed to be considered a valuable resource.

The Green Streak

A riparian area is that zone of lush green plants along the banks of a stream. In the high deserts of Idaho, these are among the few places where water is not a limiting factor. The abundant water supply allows for the development of a more varied and complex ecosystem than is found on the sagebrush desert and forms a corridor of stark contrast to the drylands it bisects.

The well-being of the riparian habitat is a key to the health of the stream that flows through it. Riparian areas are especially important in providing the thick mat of vegetation needed to stabilize the stream bank, prevent erosion, and filter out silt. The plants that grow here also serve as a buffer zone in agricultural areas. The straining action of fibrous root systems slows and reduces the movement of fertilizers and other harmful chemicals from farm fields to the stream.

Trees and shrubs of this oasis provide food and protective cover for many animals and aquatic insects during terrestrial forays. The overhanging plants benefit aquatic animals by shading the water and keeping it cool. Equally important, as these bank plants drop their foliage or die, their vegetative carcasses fall into the stream. Once in the water, the branches, leaves, and other miscellaneous parts decompose, and their energy is recycled in the form of nutrients through the entire aquatic ecosystem.

The riparian habitat along Silver Creek runs the gamut from a dynamic, diverse, natural jungle, to moderately disturbed areas that are a mishmash of native and exotic plants, to dusty, barren soil where plants are nearly non-existent. The worst of these places occur where livestock or farm equipment have eaten, trampled, or ripped out the plants over a period of many, many years.

The riparian area is seldom more than thirty yards wide on either side of Silver Creek. Often this zone is nothing more than a thicket of willows. Where more diverse, however, this green area consists of four distinct groups of plants: deciduous trees, willows, shrubs and grasses, and sedges and rushes.

On Silver Creek, the deciduous zone is limited to a few scattered stands of quaking aspen – the white- barked tree with the dark green leaves that tremble in the slightest breeze. Large groves of aspen are found in the adjacent mountains, but at lower elevations, islands of quakies are found only in locations with a good supply of water and a sandy-loam soil. This means aspen grow well in ravines or at the base of hills where streams or springs provide the water and erosion provides the soil. Only a few large stands of aspen exist along Silver Creek. The most extensive of these is the grove on the north shore of Sullivan Lake. Here, surfacing spring water and sediments deposited at the base of the Picabo Hills provide the perfect combination for aspen growth.

During the summer, there are few places that are as delightful as those beneath the canopy of a sun- splattered aspen grove. Here, the shade provides a cool habitat that supports a diverse assortment of birds. Without the aspen, cavity nesters like the mountain bluebird, common flicker, hairy woodpecker, and other birds would have few nesting sites. The aspen is also home to several species of warblers. The MacGillvary's, orange-crowned, and yellow-rumped warblers commonly search for insects and nest in the understory of the aspen forest. The crowns of these trees are also the site of a large great blue heron rookery. Numerous pairs of herons nest near Silver Creek and depend upon the shallow waters of the stream to provide the small fish they feed to their young.

Moving closer to the edge of the stream, a curtain of willows is encountered. Like the sagebrush, the willows stand alone in their ability to outcompete nearly every other plant on the stream bank. And like the sagebrush, willows are dominant because they are so well adapted to local conditions.

Willows extend their range rapidly by growing new stems from existing root systems and quickly establishing themselves in adjacent habitats. Willow thickets are a result of this type of growth. To move greater distances, willows also reproduce by seed, or when cuttings are carried cross-country by beavers. The small seeds of the willow have long hairs that help to suspend them in the air. Once airborne, the seeds can be carried by the wind to distant gravel or sand bars. These plant pioneers stabilize the bars and soon new willow tangles are born.

Although not as plentiful, there are many other shrubs that struggle to be neighbors of the willow. The red- barked chokecherry displays dozens of small, white flowers on a spike called a raceme. After these flowers bear fruit, the bright red, quarter-inch chockecherries can be collected and eaten. Terribly bitter – hence the name chokecherry – add a little sugar and you get the best jelly this side of Smuckers. A day's pickings is only a small bucketful, so someone who gives you a jar of chokecherry jelly is a true friend.

Two other common shrublike, near-trees with reddish bark are the red-stem dogwood and the water birch. The dogwood is like a strawberry plant in that it sends out runners – stems that run along or just under the ground and have the ability to send out roots that will support new growth. Water birch are small

Water Birch

trees seldom more than thirty feet in height. Since these trees only grow where water is abundant, they have very shallow root systems. With little to anchor them to the stream bank, these trees often lose their grip and slump into the stream as the bank is undercut by the current.

Smaller plants are also numerous in this luxurious, wet environment. Grasses, sedges and rushes grow in profusion. These are not the shallow rooted grasses of the sage desert. Here, the grasses form a deep- rooted lawn with extensive root masses. This lush growth can be supported because of the abundant supply of water. It is these fibrous root systems that keep the stream bank from eroding away as the stream's flow pushes into and past it.

Among these grasses are splashes of color where wildflowers are growing. The water-loving gentian, bog orchid, scarlet gilia, and wild iris are some of the flowers that are so beautiful they make you stop and ask, "What's that?" Curious circles of wild iris are found where an older plant sent out rootstalks that gave rise to younger plants. Then the parent plant dies and leaves a circle of its descendants behind.

The dense vegetation of the stream banks that provides all the necessities for numerous species of insects also attracts dozens of different birds that feed on these insects. Summertime residents include the Lazuli bunting and the warblers; the yellow, yellowthroat, and Wilson's to name a few. These are the small, nervous birds that you never get a good look at because they spend most of their time fluttering from one branch to another.

A diversion I have always enjoyed while fly fishing Silver Creek is watching the willow flycatchers. These birds perch on a branch overhanging the stream, and, like a customer at a fast-food restaurant, wait for the current to serve up a lunch of Pale Morning Duns. As the mayflies take off on their maiden flights, the flycatcher swoops down, hangs in mid-air, and snatches the bugs just as they clear the water. After feeding, the flycatcher immediately returns to its lookout post. Some of these perches are so perfect for insect hunting that they are used by flycatchers year after year.

Wild Iris

From Bank to Bank

The water of Silver Creek is like the blood pumping through your arteries. The stream must carry oxygen, chemicals, and nutrients to every living organism or they will die.

The plants that form the base of the food pyramid that supports the insects, fish, birds, and other animals that live in Silver Creek, are called "weeds" or "moss" by most anglers. To the aquatic botanist, however, the most important of these plants is chara. The most abundant plant in upper Silver Creek, chara is a freshwater alga with a preference for alkaline-rich waters. This plant grows in huge masses, and during the summer, covers about fifty percent of the stream. When compared to all other plants, chara makes up to ninety-seven percent of all plant material contained within Silver Creek.

Chara grows wherever silt covers the bottom of the stream. In early summer, chara rapidly expands into large, thick mats of vegetation. As the plant growth covers the entire stream from bank to bank, the flow of water is eventually forced to funnel its way through the green growth. As the plants restrict the movement of water to these channels, the velocity of the current increases until it creates pathways through the chara. These mini-habitats are like fast food restaurants to the fish and quickly become the trout's preferred summer hangout.

The growth of chara peaks by late summer when a phenomenon commonly known as "rollover" occurs. As the chara grows larger and larger, its dense canopy increasingly restricts

Chara

the amount of sunlight reaching the plant's stems. Since chara is an alga, the stems of this plant are composed of large cells that independently manufacture their own food. When the plant canopy limits the amount of sunlight required for photosynthesis, the lower

stems die from malnutrition and no longer have the strength to serve as a link to the rootlike fibers that anchor chara to the stream bottom. As these stems break, the chara drifts away on the current. Between rollover and the coming of the end of the growing season, much of the mat of chara disappears by late September.

The health of the chara and other aquatic plants has much to do with the abundance of other living organisms in Silver Creek. Biologists find that mayflies (Ephemeroptera), caddisflies (Trichoptera), and midges (Diptera) are the most abundant of these organisms. Researcher's have found that midges make up the largest portion of a trout's diet during the winter months, while mayflies have this undesirable honor in the summer.

Amateur entomologists (an alias for novice fly fishermen) usually make identifying adult mayflies more difficult than it really is. This occurs because anglers try to match the mayflies they pick up to the stamp sized photos found in most insect identification books. With more than 700 species of mayflies in North America, the choices can be overwhelming.

My foolproof guide to the mayflies commonly seen on Silver Creek could be written on a matchbook cover. The yellow ones that come floating by one at a time are pale morning duns (Ephemerella). Those mayflies bouncing up and down near the stream banks are speckle wings (Callibaetis). The little black and white ones that fly around in clouds are the Tricos (Tricorythodes) or white-winged blacks. Huge mayflies the size of a nickel with sandy/tan bodies are brown drakes (Ephemera). A fall hatch of mayflies with dark brown bodies and slate-gray wings is a mahogany dun (Paraleptophlebia). Anything that doesn't match these descriptions are blue-winged olives (Baetis). Later, I'll spend an entire chapter making a liar out of myself,

Green Drake Mayfly

but for most budding naturalists or fly-fishers, this system will let you identify ninety percent of the mayflies you will see on Silver Creek.

While it is the adult insects on the surface of the water that attracts our attention, biologists tell us it's the immature insect that is most important as a food source to the trout. The aquatic life stage of the mayfly is called a nymph, and these tiny, bug-eyed, mini-monsters are difficult for anyone but an expert to identify by species. In general, if any distinction between one species of nymph and another is made by a non-entomologist, the classification is usually based on the insect's behavior rather than the specifics of how many abdominal segments are covered with lateral gills, etc. Hence, nymphs are usually referred to as clingers, burrowers, swimmers or crawlers. Trout also seem happy with this simple distinction. When picking nymphs off plants, rooting for them in the gravel, or inhaling them as they swim by in the current, by plan or coincidence, the fish are acknowledging that each species of nymph lives in a very specialized habitat.

It is in trying to imitate the life cycle of the mayfly that most Silver Creek anglers go all out. Recent refinements in the sport of fly fishing now make it possible for every stage of an insect's life to be imitated. This means flies can be created to match the nymph, the emerging nymph, the trapped emerger, the dun, the adult and the spent spinner of every species of mayfly. And if having to design dozens of mayfly replicas seems a big task, remember there are plenty of other important insects here as well – like the caddisfly.

Although insects are not given much credit for deep thought, I think the ability of the caddis to design the larval cases they live in for much of their lives shows that there must be more than an occasional brainwave going through their micro-minds. No one can tell me that animals that can take small twigs and a little silk their bodies produce and build perfect, four-sided, log cabin structures don't know something about the basics of carpentry. And the caddis capable of constructing cases made entirely of sand grains, surely has a journeyman knowledge of the art of masonry. Finally, to any insect that can compute the size of mesh needed to match the speed of the current in order to weave spiderweb-like nets to trap prey, I tip my hat – neither geometry or physics were ever my better subjects.

I have to confess to ignoring the midges (Chironomidae) on Silver Creek for years, but find the more I learn about these insects the more I find myself fishing their imitations. I rely on biologists to tell me that these insects make up to seventy percent of a trout's diet during the winter and remain an important food source during the remainder of the year. According to the aquatic entomologists, immature midges live in cocoons they build in the mud. As pupa, they migrate to the surface where they break out of their skin and hatch into adults. Once on the surface, the winged adults float on the discarded pupal skin until they are strong enough to fly.

To me, midges are the insects that are always around, but rarely seen. On Silver Creek, I'm seldom sure when this hatch is taking place – I usually just assume that when nothing else is happening, midge imitations are a good bet. The best midge fishermen are those who have total confidence in imitating an insect they seldom ever see.

Some insects that are accorded only second class importance by anglers, are considered first class meals by the trout. With a lack of fast water and gravel stream bottoms, upper Silver Creek supports few stoneflies. While the little yellow stonefly (Perlodidae) is found sporadically on upper Silver Creek, those searching for the famous western hatch of western salmonflies (Pteronarcys) have to look for it on lower Silver Creek and the Little Wood River. While never found in the enormous numbers found on the streams of Yellowstone country and other famous western rivers, fishing big, black imitations of the stonefly nymph, still can entice good fish in the fast, pocket water on either of these two streams.

Other insects like damsels, dragonflies, water boatmen, riffle beetles, crane flies, leeches, water striders, and one crustacean, the scud, are also relatively abundant although few fisherman are aware of their importance. In order to fully understand the Silver Creek ecosystem and to become a better angler, every fly fisherman should spend some time identifying these other "hatches."

The biomass of bugs that is produced by the truckload is what supports the robust population of fish in Silver Creek. Originally, the only trout in this stream was the redband. At one time thought by ichthyologists to be a cutthroat trout, the redband was the native trout of the high desert and was widely distributed throughout the western United States. In studying its shrinking population, biologists have used genetic mapping to confirm that the redband is not a cutthroat, but a rainbow trout.

One of four subspecies of rainbows (Oncorhynchus mykiss gairdneri), the redband has now been so hybridized over its original range that biologists believe pure strains only exist in a few isolated places in Oregon, California and British Columbia. With the building of the Hayspur hatchery on a tributary of Silver Creek in the 1920s, trout from throughout the west were imported in an attempt to raise a high- quality trout engineered for stocking purposes. As a result, the coastal rainbow (Oncorhynchus mykiss irideus) from the McCloud River and streams in the Mount Lassen area of California as well as rainbows from Montana and Wyoming were planted at Hayspur and eventually found their way into Silver Creek. Over the years, these various species of rainbow trout either outlasted or hybridized with the redband. Eventually, the redband lineage was diluted and disappeared as a distinguishable species in Silver Creek.

Early in this century, brook trout supporters brought large numbers of this fish from its home waters of the eastern United States and dumped them into the streams of the west, including Silver Creek. Today, the higher water temperatures of lower Silver Creek restrict the brook trout to the headwaters of the stream. Brook trout compromise approximately five percent of the population on The Nature Conservancy and drop to less than two percent downstream.

Another newcomer from Europe that now resides throughout Silver Creek is the brown trout. Stocked for the first time in the Little Wood River in the 1950s, the brown eventually extended its range to the very headwaters of Silver Creek. A 1988 study found that rainbow trout made up as high as eighty-five percent of the trout population of upper Silver Creek. Brown trout made up only ten percent and brook trout the remaining five percent. In lower Silver Creek, numbers vary with the season, with rainbows comprising forty percent of the population in the fall and seventy percent in the spring. As the browns move up from the Little Wood River and into lower Silver Creek in the fall to spawn, they become dominant and make up sixty percent of the population.

Another head count done in 1992 shows that in four years the rainbow trout population has dropped by about ten percent in upper Silver Creek, while brown trout have increased by the same percentage. A similar increase in the brown trout population has been recognized on the lower section of Silver Creek.

Other species of fish found in Silver Creek include the blue-silver mountain whitefish, at least one species each of dace, suckers and the bottom-dwelling Paiute and Wood River sculpin (endemic only to the Silver Creek, Wood River and a few other nearby drainages). Because it is an isolated species that may be threatened, research is now underway to locate and identify the habitat of the Wood River sculpin.

Other animals living aquatic or semi-aquatic lives include

many species of ducks. Although mallards are the most frequently seen, the widgeon, pintail and gadwall are occasional
rewards for birders. Canada geese are very common and the
sight of a group of whistling swans flying over Silver Creek is
an incredible bonus to fishermen. Many visitors report seeing
otter and beaver on Silver Creek, and although I have never
seen a beaver, several dams, piles of wood chips, and fallen trees
found throughout the aspen groves indicate there must be at
least a few beaver families in the area. As for the otter, I have
seen a few strange wakes cutting through water at dusk, but
I've never been able to convince myself that I have seen one of
these wondrous animals.

One experience I have found unique at Silver Creek
occurred when I waded into one of the small pockets of open
water surrounded by cattails. After entering this hole in the
reeds, I could see maybe fifty feet in each direction. Because the
cattails are too tall to see over, I immediately forgot that the
rest of the world existed. This aquatic opening offered an experience very similar to entering a zoo exhibit that simulates a
particular ecosystem. At Silver Creek, this same thing can be
experienced without having to enclose everything in a cage.

I first visited one of these marsh holes when enticed inside
by the sight of a trout rising on the far side of a thin fence of
reeds. Upon entering, I saw several fish busily scooping up stationary Callibaetis spinners. With no current or wind to push
the mayflies into calm water, the fish would just casually cruise
all over the place looking for another victim to ambush. Taking
fish turned out to be easy. They hit almost anything I put in
front of them. The problem was guessing exactly where "in front
of them" was located.

When I finally had a fish stumble onto my offering, a gentle sip and a gentle set resulted in anything but a gentle
response. It was like hooking a fish in a bathtub. Five short runs
and the fish had covered every square foot of that opening.
Finally, the rainbow headed for the main stream channel. Two
feet into the wall of plants, the fish wrapped my leader tightly
around the stalk of a cattail. Tethered on six inches of tippet,
the two-pound fish was released with a flick of my forceps.

After letting the fish go, I stayed inside the ring of cattails to see if any of the other residents would begin feeding again. Standing there, I was amazed at all the activity going on around me. Yellow-headed Blackbirds with their gold facemasks held themselves in an awkward position as they perched on cattail stems. Coots, or the less complementary "mudhens," swam aimlessly, squawking at me because they had young in the area. For a brief moment, I had the opportunity to see the ducklings of this ugly, nondescript bird as they dashed out of the cover at the approach of their mother. With their dark, rusty colored heads, they were delightfully fuzzy and cute, but unfortunately as adept as their relatives at coot screeching.

As I watched all of this, a small riseform caught my attention. It wasn't a rising fish, but rather a muskrat poking around for its next meal. Since cattails are a major staple of a muskrat's diet, it didn't take the animal long to locate lunch.

With all of this activity and their brother's frantic battle still etched in their minds, the other trout in the opening chose not to expose themselves to my waiting fly. Eager to get back to stream fishing, I decided to leave the small, self-contained ecosystem. Since this experience, however, every time I come near one of these hidden communities, I poke my head in to see what the residents are up to.

Silver Creek's reputation was built upon its big, beautiful trout. Fisherman come to Silver Creek because of those big, beautiful trout. But Silver Creek deserves to be revered for much more. If you are a lawyer from Denver, Colorado, a trout bum from Bozeman, Montana, a doctor from Dallas, Texas, or just an angler from right down the road, to fully experience Silver Creek, I recommend you occasionally put your fly rod aside and watch life at its most complex – and most simple.

3
Everyone's Oasis

T he fish have always been there. They were there when the local inhabitants were nomadic Indians. They were there when the wagons arrived carrying thirsty pioneers and even thirstier oxen. And they were there when people decided that crops and livestock could be raised in this valley. Today, perhaps surprisingly, in spite of a history of water diversion, pollution, siltation, development, and just plain overuse, the fish are still here – in Silver Creek.

The Shoshone

The first person to take a fish in Silver Creek was probably just as excited as the fly fisherman who took a trout here yesterday. His ability to capture a fish made him beam with satisfaction – a pleasant sensation that was exceeded only by the anticipation of eating his trophy. The fish would go well with the pear-shaped

Idaho State Historical Society
Shoshone at Fort Hall, Idaho, 1885.

bulbs of the sego lily and chokecherries his family had gathered the day before. Added to the yellow-bellied marmot he had snared earlier that morning, this would be the best meal his family had eaten in several days.

This first fisherman was an Indian; possibly a member of the tribe now known as the Shoshone. The Shoshone home territory ranged from the canyons of the Snake River across the black, barren lava flows of the Snake River Plain, to the rugged mountains of northern Idaho. The Shoshone survived by hunting game and gathering edible plants, roots and nuts. They hunted deer, elk, and antelope with a spear thrower known as an altatl. A very lethal weapon, the altatl – a notched stick with two loops of rope fiber into which the fingers fit – was used to fling a short spear. Small game like the sage grouse and white-tailed jackrabbits were taken with bow and arrow, snare, deadfall or a well-thrown rock.

Plants, however, fed everyone when meat was in short supply. The Shoshone gathered the root of the bitterroot, which was named for its distinctive taste when eaten raw. Sunflower seeds, eaten as a snack today, could be quickly collected in great quantities. False dandelion, desert parsley and several other plants became instant salads.

To survive, the Shoshone had to ensure they had a ready and reliable supply of food during the entire year. This required planning seasonal movements very carefully. Like field workers who harvest crops as they ripen on one farm and then move on to the next, the Shoshone traveled from one of nature's bounties to another. In the early spring, they set out from the bottomlands along the Snake River just north of present-day Pocatello. Traveling north, the Shoshone crossed the forty miles or more of black-rock desert as quickly as possible. They stopped only when they located one of the widely scattered caves or lava tubes in the basalt lava flows of the Snake River Plain. The lava tubes were places where water from the winter's snowpack would collect and freeze into ice, preventing the water from passing through the porous lava. These pools of water in the dark recesses of the caves were often the only source of water to the natives in their journeys across the lava flows. The location of these waterholes was passed on from one generation to the next.

Once the Indians reached the base of the Pioneer Mountains, locating food and water was easier. With the jagged lava flows behind them, they found the traveling easier as they moved over the low foothills of the Pioneer Mountains and into the valley that contains Silver Creek. But the luxuriant oasis of Silver Creek wasn't their ultimate destination, and after only a brief stay, they moved on to their first major stop. As the Shoshone arrived at the thirty-mile long, thirty-mile wide meadow later to become known as the Camas Prairie, the camas plant was just coming into bloom. Virtually carpeting the marshy flatlands, the Shoshone harvested huge numbers of camas bulbs. The sweet, onion-like bulb could be boiled, baked, roasted or eaten raw – it was the potato of its day. In fact, when boiled, the bulb has a taste similar to a potato. To the Indians, the camas bulb insured full bellies for much of the summer.

Because of the importance of the camas to the Indians, it is easy to understand why they were so aggravated when they arrived at Camas Prairie in May, 1878. They found the area was being heavily grazed by the white man's cattle. And to the Shoshone-Bannock (the Bannock being a closely associated tribe), the final indignity was finding a band of pigs methodically uprooting one camas plant after another.

The government guaranteed the Shoshone the rights to Camas Prairie to entice them into signing a peace treaty. But when white settlers moved into the area officials took no action to remove them. Soon the Shoshone, under the leadership of Chief Buffalo Horn, took the mater into their own hands and attacked several isolated camps of herders. The U.S. Calvary was called into action when two ranchers were wounded.

What came to be called the "Bannock War" was really a lopsided tragedy. The Shoshone-Bannocks were pursued through Idaho into Oregon. Chief Buffalo Horn was killed in the very first battle. With their leader gone, the fight became a running skirmish. Soon more than 200 Indians had lost their lives, including some who had nothing to do with the incident at Camas Prairie. The war was over before the first snowfall of winter.

In the years following the war, the Shoshone lost their right to roam Camas Prairie to homesteaders and were restricted to a reservation near Pocatello. Up to that time, however, they annually arrived at the Camas Prairie in the early spring, ate their fill, and watched the prairie gradually dry up under the hot, summer sun. By July, the Indians were moving again. This time, they moved into the drainages of the Boise and Snake Rivers, where they pursued salmon returning to their spawning grounds. In strategic places along the rivers, the Shoshone built wooden weirs to funnel the salmon past platforms. The Indians on the platforms used long-handled nets to scoop the fish from the water.

The Indians followed the salmon run as far upstream as Shoshone Falls near the present day city of Twin Falls. The fish could not get past the 212-foot falls. The salmon disappeared by late summer and the Shoshone returned to the wintering grounds they had left months earlier.

So it was that the Shoshone were the first people to travel along the banks of Silver Creek. They took advantage of the bountiful population of trout found in this stream. Using the same nets, gigs and harpoons that they traditionally used to capture or skewer salmon, the Indians undoubtedly hunted trout in the small feeder streams of Silver Creek. By blocking one end of the stream with a fence of pointed willow sticks stuck into the gravel, it would have been easy for the Indians to drive the fish into the barricade and capture them.

Although fish – probably redband trout – were abundant during the period, the Shoshone were always careful to limit their take to only those fish needed to feed their family. Believing that every river had a spirit that deserved their respect, the they did their best to leave the stream unchanged. Pioneers, settlers, ranchers, real estate agents and others who followed the Shoshone often regarded the Earth and its resources differently.

The Pioneers

Pioneers, or emigrants, began moving through Idaho in the mid-1800s. Most of these travelers followed the Oregon Trail that paralleled the Snake River Canyon just south of the lava

Idaho State Historical Society
After crossing the dry, hot Snake River Plain, emigrants found
Silver Creek a welcome oasis.

fields of the Snake River Plain. For many years the Shoshone reluctantly, if not graciously, accepted the summer influx of white settlers. Just as you might be annoyed if strangers began pitching tents and camping in your back yard, the Indians eventually became infuriated with the emigrants. This was hardly a problem over a few unwelcome campers, however, because nearly 250,000 people and 1.5 million animals passed through the homeland of the Shoshone in the mid-1800s. It was nothing short of an invasion.

The Indians became more angry as they watched the horses, mules and oxen of the pioneers eat most of the grass and foul many of the waterholes. Finally, as the uninvited guests shot their game and burned their winter supply of firewood, the Shoshone saw their very survival threatened and, after years of complacency, they reacted.

The first Shoshone attack on settlers occurred at a site now managed as a state park in southern Idaho, appropriately called Massacre Rock. Only a couple of emigrants were killed in that raid on August 9, 1862, but news of the Indian uprising quickly swept through the wagon trains yet to reach Idaho. The sudden aggressiveness of the Indians made the pioneers nervous. When a mountain man named Tim Goodale offered to guide wagon trains over a trail that skirted the northern edge of the volcanic plain, well away from the area where the Shoshone were rising up and striking out, the pioneers were eager to try the new route.

This route became known as Goodale's Cutoff and veered off of the main Oregon Trail just north of Pocatello. The trail then crossed the Snake River Plain, skirting as much as possible the jagged, sharp lava flows that could cause shoe leather to disintegrate and make a horse lame in fifty yards. The reaction of the wagon drivers is summed up nicely in the 1884 journal of Julius Caesar Merrill:

> It was a desolate, dismal scenery. Up or down the valley as far as the eye could reach or across the mountains and into the dim distance the same unvarying mass of black rock. Not a shrub, bird nor insect seemed to live near it. Great must have been the relief of the volcano, powerful the emetic, that poured such a mass of black vomit.

For nearly 100 miles, the people and animals survived on the water of a few widely-scattered waterholes and, for the livestock, a few mouthfuls of grass. One can only imagine the look on the faces of man, woman and beast as they came over the foothills north of what is now the town of Carey and dropped into the lush, wet valley holding the creek that looked like silver in the light of the setting sun.

For many years, more emigrants took Goodale's Cutoff than followed the main Oregon Trail. In fact, the largest single wagon train to travel any segment of the Oregon Trail, took this route in 1864. The huge train, consisting of more than 1,100 people in at least 340 wagons, took three hours to form up and get out of camp each day.

At Silver Creek, the pioneers grazed and watered their livestock and used the sagebrush and willows for firewood. Although records are sketchy, the diaries of some of these travelers indicated they took fish to augment an otherwise bland diet of salty, dry meat and weevil-filled flour. A few of the pioneers talk about pursuing fish with hook and line, but most entries indicated snagging or spearing their prey was much more effective. Some of the pioneers even used nets to take the occasional fish dinner.

A young girl named of Annie Jane wrote in her journal:

> But the prettiest sight we seen was at Silver River (Silver Creek); there we crossed a bridge the water was ten or twelve feet deep and clear as cristle (sp). Under the bridge the fish lay on the bottom of the river side by side and looked like they do when packed for sardines. They didn't seem to be traveling. When we would make a noise some would swim away a short distance then swim right back to its place . . . They wouldn't bite a hook or pay any attention. The boys made some grab hooks and caught a few. There was large ones and small ones. The largest looked about two pounds.

Most of these pioneers quickly moved through the sage flats bordering Silver Creek. They were bound for the promised land of Oregon and had no desire to spend the winter in Idaho. But, a few families felt the land adjacent to Silver Creek was exactly what they were looking for because it provided the necessities of life.

The Settlers

The emigrants who remained by Silver Creek became farmers by necessity and soon began clearing fields for planting and digging ditches to carry irrigation water. Slowly a few log or slat-wood cabins sprang up in the valley. One enterprising individual even built a toll bridge over Silver Creek. Settlement had arrived and although there wasn't much leisure time for pursuing fish, the big trout of Silver Creek are occasionally mentioned in the writings, oral histories and photographs that remain from the early history of this area.

In the latter part of the 1800s, settlers began to farm and ranch in what was then called Silver Creek Valley. During these early years, many settlers nearly perished when icy blizzards swept through the valley. The more severe storms buried live-

Idaho State Historical Society
A typical mining operation in the Pioneer and Sawtooth mountains.

stock under snow drifts or, worse, turned the animals into
grotesque, frozen statues. Deep snow made it difficult for the
homesteaders to collect firewood needed to heat their cabins in
sub-zero weather.

For many years, the settlers considered themselves fortunate if they could raise enough food to support their family. For
those who didn't give up and move on to the more mild climate
of Oregon, it was to be some time before they could convert their
fight for survival into a profitable business. In fact, many decided that it was much easier to make their fortune in the mountains to the north, around Hailey where prospectors had discovered ores of silver and gold.

Mining and Railroads

The settlements of Ketchum, Hailey, and Bellevue were all
established to support the mining boom that took place in the
1880s. The mines of the Wood River Valley eventually produced
more than $60 million – in 1880s dollars – in gold, silver and
lead.

All of the ore mined in the Pioneer and Sawtooth

Mountains had to be hauled out of the mountains on special wagons. These narrow, very tall, wagons were designed to be attached to each other like railroad boxcars. Used in lieu of the standard, wide- box freight wagons, these wagons could better negotiate the narrow trails that lead to the mines. Up to six wagons were pulled by a string of as many as eighteen mules. They never added more mules because if they did the drivers would lose sight of the lead team as they turned sharp corners. Since the closest (at this time) railhead was located 100 miles away, at Blackfoot, Idaho, long trains of mules and wagons regularly passed through the Silver Creek area and then followed the route of Goodale's Cutoff across the Snake River Plain.

The life of the freightliners was to be short lived, however. With the development of the mines and, more importantly, the rapidly expanding population of the Big Wood River Valley, the owners of the Oregon Shortline Railroad felt that Hailey had the potential of becoming "the Denver of Idaho." In 1982, with dollar signs in their eyes, railroad entrepreneurs started building a spur line from the town of Shoshone to Hailey.

This sixty-mile section of track was called the Wood River Branch and was built by a crew of 1,000 men and 300 mules. The workers were mostly of Chinese, Irish or Italian descent. These were tough men who pushed the track forward regardless of the danger. Hardly an OSHA-approved industry, a local newspaper reported that a terrible explosion killed two workers and injured two others. Rescuers loaded the two injured survivors into the bed of a wagon and immediately set out for Bellevue for medical help. As it turned out, their wounds were not their biggest problem – both men were frozen stiff by the time they reached town!

Despite these occasional set backs, workers completed the railroad spur on May 7, 1883, when the last spike was ceremoniously driven at Hailey. Before the end of the month, the miners were shipping ore by rail. Perhaps even more significant, the trains carried passengers into the Wood River Valley on their return runs. It was to be a long time, however, before "tourism" became important in the valley. Prior to becoming a

Sheep ranching dominated the Silver Creek area until the early 1950s.

tourist mecca, residents were to see the mines go bust and agri-
culture become the backbone of the local economy.

Farming and Ranching

By the early 1900's, three small, farming settlements had
grown up on the banks of Silver Creek. Near the headwaters of
the stream was Gannett. Just downstream was Picabo. Near
the confluence of Silver Creek and the Little Wood River was
Tikura. These tiny communities served as the social hub for the
ranching and farming families scattered along the length of
Silver Creek. Today, only the towns of Picabo and Gannett still
exist.

Farmers built the first major irrigation ditch and small
canals to divert the water of the creek onto their fields and pastures in 1881. The most extensive of these was Kilpatrick's
Ditch, which was constructed on the south side of Silver Creek.
Water supplied by this diversion canal allowed homesteaders to
irrigate wild hay, grain and, eventually, alfalfa. When the harvest of these crops made it possible to supplement the grass
available in the nearby mountain meadows during the spring

and summer, some of the farmers turned to ranching as well. Most ranchers chose to raise sheep.

Picabo became a wool-shearing center for all of central Idaho. At one time, herders brought over a hundred thousand sheep into this small town each year. Picabo's population peaked at 250 people in 1932. As each herd was trailed into town, dust billowed high into the air. Old timers speak about being able to keep track of incoming herds by counting the clouds of dust in the distance.

Sheep ranching dominated the Silver Creek area until the early 1950s. Then a large drop in consumption of lamb and higher production costs contributed to a nation-wide decline in the sheep industry. Production figures show that from 1942 to 1951, the number of sheep raised in the United States declined by forty-three percent. These developments caused a shift to cattle raising in the Wood River Valley and the growing of alfalfa and other profitable crops such as oats, wheat and barley.

Recreation

There are few references that discuss the recreational opportunities of Silver Creek in the early 1900s. This is probably because local people considered fishing more like work than fun. When people talked about having a good time, they were referring Fourth of July gatherings, debates, and taking a dunk at the local swimming hole. A few photographs from this period, however, show there was some fishing taking place on Silver Creek.

These photos showed men – never women – holding the ends of long cords from which they had suspended large catches of fish. Local court records indicate that some of these men were found guilty of "selling of fish for commercial purposes", so it is easy to conclude that not everyone looked at fishing as a sport.

The development of the recreation potential of Silver Creek was to await the tourism boom that began in the 1930s. While searching for a site to build a ski resort to rival those in Europe, Averell Harriman, owner of the Union Pacific Railroad, eventually focused on the mountainous area surrounding Ketchum. Here, Harriman built the first destination ski resort in the

This monument near Sun Valley honors the area's most famous writer and sportsman, Ernest Hemingway.

United States. Developers called the resort Sun Valley, a name meant to attract skiers by emphasizing the warmth of the lodge rather than the cold of the ski slopes. After the installation of the first chair lift – based on a design for a conveyor belt to load bananas on ships – Sun Valley became a premier vacation spot.

The Sun Valley Inn was an instant draw for celebrities. Film Director David O. Selznick, accompanied by actresses Joan Bennet and Claudett Colbert, attended the grand opening of the resort. Over the years, celebrities such as Gary Cooper, Ingrid Bergman, John Wayne, Clark Gable, and Jackie Kennedy came to Sun Valley. More recently, Demi Moore, Bruce Willis, Arnold Schwarzenegger, and Clint Eastwood have chosen to become regular visitors to the Wood River Valley.

Perhaps the most famous celebrity of all, writer Ernest Hemingway, first came to Sun Valley in 1939. Although he never stayed too long in one place, Hemingway became enamored by the beauty of Idaho's mountains and its sagebrush plains. While working on his book, *For Whom the Bell Tolls*, Hemingway managed to find plenty of time for hunting. One of his favorite spots was Silver Creek, where he found ducks to be plentiful.

Although the public relations people of the ski resort circulated photos to the press of Hemingway displaying fish he supposedly caught on Silver Creek, he did very little fishing in the area. Monster marlin, sleek sailfish, and other big-game fish were his passion, not trout.

After building ski runs, lodges and swimming pools in Sun Valley, Averill Harriman looked for new ways to increase the attractiveness of the resort. Managers were especially interested in expanding their season into

Deserted cabins on Silver Creek.

the summer and fall months. In 1940, the railroad company purchased two ranches located at the headwaters of Silver Creek. They renamed their property the Sun Valley Ranch, a place for guests who wanted to fish for Silver Creek trout in the summer and hunt ducks that arrived in the fall.

Preferring to keep any development to a minimum, only two primitive cabins and a dog kennel were built near Sullivan Lake (named for the ranch's previous owner). These rustic accommodations provided the basic necessities for both guests and guides. And, except for providing periodic grazing for the resort's saddle horses, the agricultural potential of the land was completely ignored.

A new ranch foreman changed the situation in the early 1950s. Then, nearly every parcel of tillable land adjacent to Silver Creek went into cultivation. With profits as the guiding force, cattle ranching soon followed. It would be several years, but eventually this intensive farming would put the future of Silver Creek and its fishery in jeopardy.

Just when Silver Creek's reputation as a very special fishing stream originated is difficult to determine. Up until the 1950s, few people traveled long distances to fish Silver Creek, but local fishermen knew it as a stream where you could catch a bunch of big fish to take home for dinner. Most of these fishermen tried to entice Silver Creek trout with night crawlers or a single salmon egg drifted through the deep channels between the weed beds. Anglers also considered a small flatfish weighted with a split shot as a hot lure when fished on a casting rod.

There was an occasional fly fisherman on the stream, but the equipment they used was very different from that available today. Fishermen used fiberglass or bamboo rods and had to dress their fly lines with floatant. Small diameter tippets were still unknown and anglers found the light leaders available entirely too fragile to hold a good fish. Fly selection was limited to what we now call classic or traditional patterns: Adams, Ginger Quill, Light Cahill, and Mosquito. At this time, a small fly was a size 14.

Regardless of equipment or technique, fishermen must have done rather well because, even then, anglers complained that there were always a lot of other fishermen on the stream. A bag limit that allowed for the taking of ten fish indicated that the fish managers must also have felt trout were abundant. The trout taken were good size; anglers judged a nice fish as one in the three to six pound (nineteen to twenty-inch plus) range.

Deterioration

The farming operations that sprouted, or expanded along the banks eventually began to impact the aquatic habitat at Silver Creek. The average size of a large fish shrank to less than two pounds (fifteen inches) and there was a significant drop in the number of fish being caught. Fishermen began to report that the flow of water in Silver Creek was decreasing as more and more wells pumped irrigation water to the surface. As new land was plowed to allow additional crops to be planted, greater amounts of top soil made its way into the stream.

Another significant threat to the stream, was posed by local farmers who drained the expansive marshes that bordered Silver Creek and put the land into cultivation. These marshes caught much of the blowing dust before it reached the stream and, with the disappearance of these buffers, siltation increased even more rapidly.

The biggest problem in Silver Creek was caused by low-water conditions and a gradual increase in the buildup of silt. The silt formed a deep mud that buried the trout's spawning

Silver Creek was an essential resource for early farms, but fertilizers, pesticides and overgrazing by livestock dramatically altered the stream.

areas and forced out existing plants and insects, while greatly altering the environment and changing the stream's ecology.

Silt also became a significant problem at the Hayspur Hatchery on Loving Creek. In order to keep the hatchery's raceways clean, managers found it necessary to install baffles and cleaning systems that removed tons of sediment each month. Because of the buildup of sediment in Silver Creek, anglers began to spend more and more time on the feeder streams – Stalker, Grove, and Loving Creeks – where the fishing was better. Eventually, the effects of heavy siltation spread into these waters as well.

By the late 1960s, the number of trout in the Silver Creek watershed had begun to decline. Those fish that remained resembled thin-bodied snakes. Recognizing that the fishing was deteriorating rapidly, the Idaho Department of Fish and Game dropped the limit of trout that could be taken to six per day. The regulations also allowed only two fish of more than sixteen inches in length to be included in the bag limit.

Silver Creek's reputation as a first class fishery began to wain as the accumulative effects of siltation, water diversion, pesticides, fertilizers, and overgrazing dramatically altered the stream. It is easy to blame the farmers and ranchers of the Silver Creek Valley for causing all of these problems, but that would be wrong. Most of these people, with the exception of a few that were either very ignorant or very greedy, appreciated Silver Creek as much or more than the fishermen. After all, the stream was their lifeblood in this otherwise bone-dry valley. The problems instead should be laid on the altar of progress. Like most Americans, they adopted new technology and overdosed on it while Silver Creek deteriorated as a fishery and an aquatic resource because of it.

The impacts of certain farming, ranching techniques were soon seen throughout the entire Silver Creek ecosystem. The damage was reversible, however. Changes for the better started when the Union Pacific decided to get out of the ski resort business and sold the Sun Valley Resort in 1964.

The new resort owner of the Sun Valley Company, Bill Janss, quickly recognized the drastic overgrazing that had taken place on the Sun Valley Ranch and immediately removed the cattle. This, along with a change to more sustainable farming practices, turned out to be the first of several important decisions that put Silver Creek on the path to recovery.

Change and The Nature Conservancy

In 1975, when the Sun Valley Company decided to sell its ranch, developers began drooling. But before the stream could be put on the auction block, a small group of Silver Creek devotees (open access to this section of Silver Creek had been allowed for many years) contacted Jack Hemingway – son of Ernest Hemingway and an Idaho Fish and Game Department Commissioner – and asked him if there was some way this land could be saved.

In turn, Hemingway contacted The Nature Conservancy, an environmental group with a growing reputation for acquiring threatened habitats. The Nature Conservancy, ignoring the reputation Silver Creek had for being "just a rich man's fishing hole," agreed to lead a campaign to raise the large amount of money needed to purchase the Sun Valley Ranch.

Every fly fisherman who has since cast a fly on this stream

owes a debt to The Nature Conservancy, Jack Hemingway, world famous angler Ernest Schwiebert, and the hundreds of fishermen, sportsmen, photographers, guides, bird watchers, and canoe paddlers who worked to raise the money needed to purchase the original 479 acres that became the Silver Creek Preserve. But money was only part of the solution. Much more important was managing this incredible resource into the future.

Founded in 1951, today The Nature Conservancy is a non-profit organization that

The Nature Consrvancy has played a critical role in the effort to restore Silver Creek.

manages the largest system of private sanctuaries in the world. In each of their distinct preserves, the primary goal of The Nature Conservancy is to safeguard plants and animals by protecting their habitats.

Originally, The Nature Conservancy saw its role as raising funds to quickly purchase key parcels of habitat – primarily within the United States – as they came up for sale. Their strategy was to buy these lands to keep them out of the hands of private developers and then donate them to various state and federal agencies. The transfer of ownership of these special lands was to take place as soon as the government organizations were ready to accept managerial and financial responsibility for the area.

In recent times, however, the public funding needed to manage these areas seldom materialized. This situation eventually caused The Nature Conservancy to develop their own teams of resource managers and biologists to oversee the lands they have acquired. As a result, The Nature Conservancy gradually built a staff of professionals that rivals those found in state and federal systems. The Nature Conservancy now employs a work force of experts capable of making their own decisions on how these sites can best be restored and preserved for the future.

This was the exact scenario that took place at Silver Creek. Since adopting the stream, The Nature Conservancy, in cooperation with the Idaho Department of Fish and Game, Idaho's universities, local farmers and ranchers, and a small army of volunteers, has initiated many programs to help restore the habitat at Silver Creek. Catch-and-release restrictions have been established on upper Silver Creek, and a reduced bag limit has been established for other sections of the stream. Idaho State University has sponsored research that established baseline inventories of plants and animals and examined many different facets of Silver Creek. But many problems still remain. We continue to ask too much of this stream.

Too Many Anglers

A lot of people come to fish Silver Creek. In recent years, thousands of visitors – each wanting to use some portion of the Silver Creek Preserve – annually sign the log book at the cabin that serves as the stream's headquarters and visitor center. With the U.S. Forest Service projecting the demand for outdoor recreation to increase by as much as eighty percent by the year 2030, managers can only expect the number of users at Silver Creek to increase dramatically with each passing decade.

It is this rapid rise (a more than tenfold increase over the last twenty years) in the number of anglers and other users that Silver Creek manager consider the Preserve's major problem. Because of this concern, Preserve managers first asked researchers in the 1980s to determine effect of Silver Creek's growing popularity. First, their study was to determine if the increase in number of encounters with other recreationists during the typical day on Silver Creek was adversely affecting the quality of the experience for some users? Secondly, what impacts were the increasing hordes having on the habitat? And finally, if the answer to either of the first two questions was yes, what action should The Nature Conservancy take to mitigate the problems?

In a nutshell, the answer to the first question about over-crowding was a definite yes – and no. When a statistical analysis was done of the answers to a survey given to users, the number of contacts with other visitors matched what respondents had identified as a level acceptable in providing the satisfactory experience they were seeking. On the other hand, when asked outright if they felt the preserve was too crowded, the majority of respondents said yes to this question.

This conflict may well have been the result of angler's and other user's perception of what constitutes an ideal visit. The presence of other visitors at The Nature Conservancy was still, for most users, below the threshold where an enjoyable experience would no longer be attainable. Indeed, the researchers concluded that visitation at the time of the study (approximately 8,000 users per year) had only recently begun to approach the levels at which people find it impossible to enjoy the type of experience they came to Silver Creek to enjoy. The researchers warned, however, that "in order to satisfy the majority of visitors, managers should attempt to keep visitor numbers below 100 per day."

In response to the second question about impacts on the environment, again the biologists came up with a "yes and no" answer. Yes, the high use of the streamside areas was leading to the undesirable creation of numerous common trails and the trampling of some vegetation. No, within most of the preserve, visitor impacts were not yet at a level considered unacceptable for a recreational area.

For the time being, it seemed the problem of the number of users reaching unacceptable levels wouldn't occur because of self-regulation. Put simply, it was found that those visitors who valued solitude or at least desired a minimum amount of contact with other fishermen, were already starting to shy away from Silver Creek. As a result, total visitation saw only a moderate annual growth through the early 1990s. By 1996, however, visitation jumped considerably to reach 12,000 users per year. At this level, earlier conclusions about visitor satisfaction and impacts on the environment may well be invalid.

Today, the cattail marsh in the area of Silver Creek known as the S-curves has had to be closed to use because it had become a maze of trails stomped through the reeds. Today, fishermen talk about near fistfights caused when one angler moves into what another angler sees as his territory. And today, we see signs posted in the fall asking fishermen to start fishing after 10 A.M. to avoid conflicts with early morning duck hunters.

As use soars, The Nature Conservancy is beginning to review its options. The Nature Conservancy staff is unanimous in feeling that if the biological health of the preserve is being jeopardized then radical steps may have to be taken. At the time being, the ramifications and effectiveness of limiting use through rod limits, reservations, a first-come-first- served system, or some combination of these controls are all being considered.

The requirement that anyone fishing the Silver Creek Preserve be a member seems destined for implementation in the near future. This policy would probably reduce the number of fishermen on the preserve section of Silver Creek and, at the same time, help to raise some of the funding needed to operate the Preserve and carry out necessary projects.

To reduce visitor impact on the vegetative communities in this area, the Conservancy has constructed a limited number of trails, boardwalks, and bridges to reduce the effects that several hundred pairs of lugged-bottomed hiking shoes and several thousand pairs felt-soled, wading boots are having on heavily used locations within this fragile landscape. They also plan to promote the wider dispersal of users along the entire length of the Silver Creek drainage system.

The Nature Conservancy may also need to make more delicate or severely overused areas off-limits to visitors. This practice is becoming more common in heavily used recreational areas like the national parks.

Finally, The Nature Conservancy intends to develop an educational program for all users. Although a subtle program now, if users don't soon understand the meaning of "minimal

Researchers pump the stomach of a brown trout.

impact" and develop an understanding of how to properly treat particularly sensitive sites, a more direct approach may be needed.

Too Many Brown Trout

Some fishermen are very upset that the brown trout, a fish they believe to be a voracious predator, has established itself in Silver Creek. These anglers believe the brown trout is quite capable of bringing about the extinction of the more acrobatic rainbow that they prefer to catch. Other fishermen welcome brown trout because they feel it adds another aspect to the variety of the fishing experiences Silver Creek offers.

In this mini-controversy, some guides dislike brown trout because they believe the techniques needed to catch these fish are beyond the ability most of their clients have mastered. Other guides look upon the brown as a special prize that serves as a worthy reward for an angler willing to pass up large pods of rainbows feeding on the surface to take on the challenge of trying to lure a big brown from beneath an undercut bank.

Some biologists dislike brown trout because it is a true exotic species, reaching the United States from Europe in the 1800s. These biologists believe the brown trout is now competing with rainbow trout and other native fish for the stream's resources. Other biologists feel the ancestries of both the brown trout and the current species of rainbow trout are both at variance with the stream's original resident – the redband trout. Some biologists also believe that brown and rainbow trout occupy very different niches within the spring creek habitat so that competition is kept to a minimum and both species lead a harmonious existence.

The brown trout was well established in lower Silver Creek by the late 1970s. For many years, small, wooden dams blocked access upstream and the brown was unable to extend its range into the headwaters of Silver Creek. It appears that in the late 1970s, a few brown trout were released above the barricades and spread throughout the upper Silver Creek drainage.

Recently, fishery biologists from Idaho State University have been looking at the results of the brown trout's arrival in upper Silver Creek. Their early observations are: 1) the brown trout population is well established, but they are presently outnumbered by rainbow trout by nearly four to one, 2) examination of stomach contents of browns indicate rainbow fingerlings are occasionally eaten but that bridgelip suckers and whitefish make up by far the largest portion of the fishes diet, 3) the brown trout spend most of their time holding in isolated pockets of deep water, while rainbow trout prefer to cruise shallow water looking for prey.

The data seems to show that brown trout have at least a moderate impact on the rainbow trout population. But the scientists would be the first to withhold a final judgement until more research has been completed. For now, when a fishermen, guide, or amateur ecologist speaks of lifting the catch and release restrictions and allowing the brown trout to be killed for the good of Silver Creek, an equal number of fishermen, guides and amateur ecologists look at them with a horrid look of disbelief.

Too Much Silt

Silt enters a stream when cattle pulverize the streamside while drinking, when stream banks cave in because the willows have disappeared and no longer hold the soil in a maze of roots, and when the wind blows across fallow fields and picks up dust that later falls into the stream. At Silver Creek, the thickness of the silt indicates all of these events have had an impact on the aquatic ecosystem. The silt has buried many of the stream's gravel bottoms and greatly reduced suitable spawning areas for fish. The thick mud has altered the type of plants that live in the stream. And the decaying ooze has

A dredge removes silt from Stalker Creek.

changed the distribution of many aquatic insects.

By changing farming practices, eliminating cattle use, and replacing native vegetation, The Nature Conservancy is beginning to have some success in eliminating much of the siltation problem. A much greater challenge may be the task of removing deposits that have built up over many years. A "muck vacuum cleaner" has been tested in heavily silted areas on upper Stalker Creek. Here, water and silt were pumped out of the middle of the stream and onto adjacent fields.

Early evaluations of the results of pumping indicate immediate improvement is seen when silt is removed from ponds or areas of heavy siltation and that downstream areas often clear quickly after silt is removed from these ponds. Apparently, when silt is removed from the slow water areas that are filled to a maximum with the material, it immediately begins to accumulate once more. While this means that the ponds will eventually refill with silt, areas where the water is flowing faster will be benefited for quite some time.

Currently, the managers of The Nature Conservancy feel that if silt was removed at several selected sites, the health of the entire stream would greatly improve. Further work in this area is planned as funding becomes available.

Too Many Cattle

A cow's idea of cattle heaven is a cool stream wandering through a smorgasbord of tasty shrubs and melt-in-your mouth grass. So, who can blame a cow for setting up home in the middle of an island of lush vegetation when they have free access to a stream? The problem is that cattle are not afraid to eat themselves out of house and home.

When cattle are not kept out of riparian areas, they eat and stomp stream bank plants until they disappear. This sets up an ugly chain of events:

• Denuded banks erode easily and tumble into the stream to add to siltation problems.
• As the stream expands into its banks, it becomes wider and shallower, allowing the water to warm.
• As overhanging plants disappear, the hot sun shines directly onto the stream all day long and warms the water even more.

A few years of unrestricted, heavy grazing and bang! – willows and grass have been replaced by mud and worthless, exotic thistles – fingerlings disappear as trout fail to spawn – big trout float belly up in mid- summer when water gets too warm and oxygen levels drop. If left unchecked, what was a diverse, efficient, energy-balanced, self-sustaining ecosystem becomes a cowpie-lined ditch.

The Nature Conservancy has launched a very aggressive program to solve the cattle problem, or better, the loss of stream bank vegetation problem. Cattle have been removed from Conservancy property and staff members have been working with local ranchers by fencing out cattle along the much of the remainder of the stream. These actions have been followed by massive planting of willows, river birch, and other native plants along the banks of Silver Creek. Since 1992, The Nature Conservancy has worked with volunteers to plant more than 10,000 of these shrubs and trees. The effort is not only restoring the riparian habitat, but serving as motivation for every landowner to take a close look at the condition of their own stream banks.

Too Many Parasites

Whirling disease, the infection that attacks and eventually kills juvenile salmonoids, was first discovered in the Silver

Creek drainage in 1988. The infected fish were found in Loving Creek near Hayspur Hatchery.

In 1995, whirling disease was discovered again in the hatchery at Hayspur and in Stalker Creek. This lead to a study being initiated in 1995 to determine the potential this problem might have on Silver Creek in the future.

Preliminary results from the study indicate that although whirling disease exists in Silver Creek, trout displaying the symptoms of the disease have not been observed. According to the final report, "whirling disease is not a threat to the trout resources in the Preserve." Hopefully, the lack of individual fish observed with the disease (as the trout's cartilage is destroyed it cause the fish to swim like a dog chasing its tail) means it is having little impact on the trout in Silver Creek and conditions may be such that it may never be a threat to the health of the fish.

Too Much Thirst

The people of Silver Creek and Wood River Valleys have probably never felt they have had all the water they needed. Shortages caused by periods of droughts (especially in the 1930s), the constant expansion of agricultural lands, and the steady increase in population all required additional water. Like everywhere in the arid west, this increasing demand for water has the potential to be the single, most unsurmountable problem local citizens will face in the future.

Over the years, many farmers decided that, if irrigated, that a marginal forty acres of sage-covered land they owned would produce enough alfalfa to pay for another year of college for the kid. Other people determined – after one drive-by shooting too many – that it was time to pull up stakes in California, retire to the banks of the Big Wood River, and build that dream house with three full baths, a hot tub and a professional-size putting green. Still others felt rolling lawns and miniature lakes were just the thing to dress up multi-million dollar housing developments.

The water supply began to dwindle, but the drop in water flow occurred so slowly that the problem wasn't perceived as serious. Then came the drought that lasted for eight years (1987 to 1994).

For year after year, southern Idaho experienced dry winters – eighty – then sixty – then forty percent of normal snowfall. Praying for water brought little results and cloud seeding couldn't provide and relief because it doesn't work if there aren't any clouds. Only when the crops and wildflowers began turning brown by June did people finally realize that, without water, there can be no life in a high desert.

But westerners are a stubborn lot and when they couldn't get enough water from the stream, looked at other alternatives; they could reduce the amount of water they used to water their crops or find another source of water – a source such as ground water. A technique that combined the best of both of these choices, center-pivot, sprinkler systems soon became a popular method for watering crops. As these sprinklers pivoted around like the minute hand of a watch, they twitched and sprayed water in a huge circle and, farmers found that as their cost for labor dropped, their crop yield increased.

In the 1980s, the number of these watering systems that tapped into the underground aquifer replaced flood irrigation on more and more farms – in 1975 thirteen percent of the area was irrigated by sprinklers, today, seventy-four percent are watered with this method. Today, the number of sprinkler systems in the area is fast approaching one hundred.

But as crops continued to flourish and expand, the downside was that Silver Creek suffered. First, much of the ground water that would eventually surface at Silver Creek, was being tapped and brought to the surface. Secondly, the canal water once used to flood irrigate farm fields was now being pumped into the sprinklers and sprayed onto the surface. Water that had once seeped into the soil to eventually reappear in Stalker, Loving, Grove, and Silver Creek now evaporated before penetrating into the ground. It is this combination of water lost to the atmosphere, an increase in water use, and the effects of a severe drought that have combined to rob Silver Creek of much of its precious liquid. In 1994, the amount of water flowing in Silver Creek reached an all time record low.

The Conservancy is trying to head off further loss of water

to prevent future catastrophic results. Currently, The Nature Conservancy is driving a study to develop a model of water use and movement in the Wood River and Silver Creek Valleys. The staff of The Conservancy are also developing programs to educate both children and adults in the disastrous impacts they are having on an irreplaceable resource. Probably most importantly, however, is that the drought broke during the winter of 1994-95 with an above normal snowpack accumulating in the area This was followed by an average snowpack in 1995- 1996 and a snowfall well above normal in 1996- 1997. If there is one place the battle for an environmental treasure can be won in Idaho, I feel it is at Silver Creek. Why, because The Conservancy is getting the word out – this isn't a case of which people will win and who will lose, its a case of everyone winning or everyone losing.

While I support the philosophical goals of most environmental organizations, I feel that most such groups spend much of their energy in attempting to increase membership, expanding facilities, or participating in less-than-effective political bickering. The Nature Conservancy seems to be different – it seems to have the ability to stay focused on its primary reason for existing – to save entire ecosystems before they are beyond hope. If we have to rely on any one group to preserve and save Silver Creek for the future, The Nature Conservancy may be our best chance. So far the fish of Silver Creek have survived the Indian's traps, the pioneer's nets, the cow's appetite, the crippling effects of a parasite, and the meat-hunter's stringer. I have faith they will survive us as well.

Will Silver Creek Survive Our Heavy Boots?

In a report to The Nature Conservancy in 1980, Spencer B. Beebe, a past manager of the Silver Creek Preserve wrote:

"The technology of identifying and acquiring natural area land is well understood. But we not only don't know what the technology of real stewardship is, we are still groping with the philosophical and conceptual framework within which to develop the technology. Sometimes it seems the only way to start is to require everyone going to Conservancy Preserves to go barefoot the way one enters a Japanese house. After a few centuries of "Barefoot in the Preserve," we may begin to understand the distinction between participation and use.

There is certainly no point in waiting for the government to explore these ideas. The voting majority is not apt to leave its shoes behind. It is too tough a path; collectively we tend to opt for the easy way out than the rough way in."

The staff at Silver Creek has framed this quote and hung it in the john that adjoins their office. In this place of honor, they can occasionally contemplate its message and further ponder the difficulty of preserving a habitat we seem to be loving to death.

4
Fishing Challenges

Silver Creek gets a lot of notice. Every year, the stream is touted by angling experts on several Saturday morning television programs, is the main program at dozens of monthly trout-club meetings, and is the focus of several fly-fishing or outdoor magazine articles. In each of these presentations, Silver Creek is made out to be a magical fly fishing nirvana where big-bellied trout feast on hatches that are measured by the size of the cloud they make. And, although it is said in reverence, the stream is often referred to as every fly fisherman's nightmare; a slow-motion stream where trout have forever to scrutinize a fly drifting in a liquid with the clarity of distilled water. Here if a mayfly has three tails, then the tail on your imitation had better be tied using three filaments, not two.

So Silver Creek has the reputation of having the perfect combination of large, dependable hatches and abundant trout that are too finicky to be taken by any but the well-skilled angler. Is Silver Creek the superbowl of fly fishing or is its fame based on hype? As a fisherman who has fished most of the more famous trout streams of the west, I'd say Silver Creek is an, honest-to-God, true challenge for any fly-fisher. In fact, Silver Creek presents the angler with a whole array of interesting challenges.

The Challenge of Selective Trout

Many authors who write about fishing don't give trout much credit for intelligence. Every analysis of a trout's cranial capacity starts with a similar statement – "With the brain the size of a pea, our quarry is at a marked disadvantage." I guess if you're going to base it on brain mass, then we should all be able to outwit 500 trout for every one that gets the best of us. Not hardly.

I agree that trout don't know how to tie a leader to a fly line or understand the fishing regulations of Idaho, but then they don't need to. Besides mating – and we all know how much brain power that takes — all they need to do is find, and keep from becoming, dinner. In the trout's world, the fish that can pick the most goodies from the aquatic conveyor belt of life while never falling for a feathered fake, wins.

But some writers do admit that the trout of Silver Creek may be just a bit more difficult to catch. After all, these trout are what fly fishermen call "selective." Some authors define selectivity as the conscious choice of a fish to feed on the insect that will provide the maximum amount of food while requiring the minimum expenditure of energy to catch. Others writers view selectivity as a trout's natural preference for a certain insect or the tendency for trout to form a "search image" for identifying first rate-meals or, in some cases, the snacks to be avoided because they contain hidden hooks. For those of us who don't seem to have as much insight into the motivations of a trout, selective fish are simply the ones that are hard to catch.

It seems that selectivity is only common in fish that have an easy life. A trait found only in fish that can afford to pass up one mouthful after another and still not starve to death. Since few place provides better living conditions – abundant insects and dillydallying currents – than Silver Creek, these trout can get away with being discriminatory and become extremely critical. These are fish that, in the words of Clint Eastwood, are "your worst nightmare". To catch these fish, the first challenge for the fly fisherman is to figure out is "What is on the menu?"

The Menu

When you arrive at the stream, stifle that urge to immediately begin flinging flies. Take at least a few minutes to just observe what the aquatic insects are doing. Most of the time, it will be easy to identify any ongoing, major hatches. But don't make any assumptions. If the mayflies are obviously pale morning duns, capture a few to determine if they are size 16, 18, or 20. If there are Baetis on the water, catch some and determine their exact size and color. Without gluing a mayfly to your hook, you will never create an exact copy, but it never hurts to come as close as possible.

Since it is remarkably difficult to capture mayflies that are floating on the current, you should always carry a small dip net like those used to catch guppies in an aquarium. For flying insects, I have found that using my hat as a sweep net is a fairly effective means of capturing them on the wing. If you're serious about knowing what insects are floating or swimming in the water, then a small seine is also needed to sample the underwater flow. I find that slipping the leg from an old pair of panty hose over my net works great for catching mayflies, midges, and anything else below the surface.

If no hatch is taking place, just stand in the stream and watch the water just upstream of your position. Dip out whatever comes by – short-legged beetles, long-legged striders, and the tiny, little black things that don't seem to have any legs at all – and examine them. Wander over by the edge of the stream and see what insects are being carried by the current next to the bank. Here, if they are active, there should be a much higher number of terrestrials – beetles, hoppers, ants – than in the middle of the stream. There may also be slack water areas along the bank where spent spinners from a recent hatch are still floating, waiting for a trout to harvest them.

To be effective, the observation of insects must be done repeatedly throughout the day and from week to week. Just as a cafe's menu changes with breakfast, lunch and dinner, so does the stream's offering of insects over the course of a day and with each passing week. Watching the insects and the trout's response to them is always characteristic of successful Silver Creek anglers.

Selecting the Main Course

Once it has been determined what insects are available to the trout, the next challenge is determining exactly which insect or stage of insect the fish are feeding on. Some anglers feel that the trout will be taking the largest, relatively abundant, insect available. Others assume it is best to always imitate the most abundant insect regardless of its size. Still others say the key is to identify the most vulnerable insect – the one easiest for the trout to capture. At any given time, each of these approaches may work on certain fish, most of the fish or, unfortunately, none of the fish. Three things can increase your odds of identifying the insect the trout are feeding on – regular, constant observation, experience, and persistence.

During a good hatch, the first step in identifying what trout are feeding upon is to figure out if the majority of the fish are taking insects above or below the surface. Splashy, sipping, or rolling rises that leave bubbles floating on the surface are telltale evidence that the trout has taken air into its mouth during the rise and prove the trout are readily taking insects on top of the water. On the other hand, bulging rises where only a trout's dorsal fin breaks the surface may indicate nymphs are being taken just prior to emergence. A lack of rising fish may not be evidence that trout aren't feeding, but rather that they are finding it more effective to take nymphs or some other underwater organism well below the surface.

Other rise types are also indicative of what a fish is feeding on. A trout that breaks through the surface in such a rush that it launches itself into the air may be pursuing a mayfly that lifted off the water at the last second. But if caddis are hatching, it is more likely that the trout is going after a caddis fly as it rockets from the water into flight. In a bulging rise, where a trout's back then tail break the surface of the water, fish are typically taking nymphs rising to the surface. A less aggressive fish, however, may take these same nymphs by merely holding just below the surface. Then as a nymph struggles to reach the surface, the trout slowly rises so that its dorsal fin and tail are sticking out of the water like the periscope and control tower of a submarine. Then with its fins poking above the surface, the trout siphons up the nymphs just before they hatch. Fish that feed in this manner find it easier to take the insects underwater than to risk missing the floaters that get airborne so quickly.

A fish waving its tail in the air in shallow water, indicates the trout is scavenging for nymphs on the bottom. This is not common on Silver Creek, but I have observed trout doing this as they root around in either silt, gravel or weed beds like pigs looking for corncobs in the mud.

When only one species of mayfly is hatching, it can be difficult to decide whether a fish is feeding on nymphs, emergers, duns or spinners. On a day in late July when it is easy to find places on the stream where several species of mayflies, grasshoppers, winged-ants, small black caddis, beetles, and damselflies on the water at the same time, identifying what each fish is feeding becomes nearly impossible. During these multiple emergences, I have observed only two types of trout – those that concentrate and feed on one specific insect at a specific stage of development and those that take any living thing that floats by. Those trout that eat everything are no problem. The extremely picky ones are God's special little gift to over-confident anglers.

One of the best methods to determine what trout are eating during multiple hatches is to use a stomach pump – I mention this with some reservations because it has always bothered me to do this to a fish that I hope to come back and catch again some day. During surgery, I have had tubes stuck down my gullet and it has never been one of my favorite things. Hopefully, when done right (syringe is filled with water, cautiously inserted into the fish's stomach, water slowly squeezed into the fish, water and stomach contents are gently sucked out) siphoning stomach contents doesn't harm the fish. The biggest difficulty in using this method is that it is first necessary to catch a fish!

It is always best to meet the challenge of selective trout by basing the selection of your fly on careful surveillance followed by detailed analysis. But if this fails, remember one of the most popular fly patterns ever used on Silver Creek is the "What-the-hell- nothing-else-works."

Other Challenges

Once you have the ability to determine what offering might most interest a trout, you face the challenge of how to best imitate a speck of living biomaterial so small that it can only be seen clearly with a magnifying glass. The demands are clear: 1) select a fly capable of fooling a fish, 2) present the fly so that it

mimics the exact behavior of the real thing, and 3) get the fly
into the trout's feeding lane without frightening the fish.

Entire books could be and have been written on what goes
through the heads of fishermen as they contemplate which fly
choice will work best. Selection can be as simple as utilizing the
fly the clerk at a sporting goods store recommends or just rely-
ing on the pattern that worked the last time you fished this particular hatch. Generally, since at least some thought has gone
into the selection of an appropriate fly, either of these approaches will produce at least a few fish.

The next step – developing the perfect fly for every circum-
stance – quite honestly, produces very few additional fish for the
amount of time that must be spent watching insects and later
at the fly tying bench. But for those willing to dedicate themselves to perfecting and customizing their flies, it's not the
catching of more fish that is the reward, but rather being able
to fool the fish that other anglers can't get to even look at their
fly. Nothing is more satisfying than, after having your fly
ignored, taking a fish the first time you cast out a slightly different pattern that you designed and tied yourself.

Once you are convinced that you have the perfect pattern,
being able to correctly imitate the behavior of the insect with
your fly becomes much more than just deciding if a fly should
be dead drifted on the surface or slowly stripped back under
water. Presentation involves the utmost attention to how
insects act during the various stages of their life cycle and being
able to portray the naturals exactly as they appear to the lurk-
ing trout. For many years, I have carried a glass petri dish in
my vest. After filling it with water, I can drop any insect (or fly)
into it and, by looking up through the bottom, determine exactly what an insect (fly) looks like from a trout's perspective.

While I realize that viewing an insect floating in a glass
dish full of water is not quite the real thing, it does give me a
good idea of what the fish sees without having to join it on the
bottom of the stream. This method has shown me that traditional hackled flies have way too many "legs," that live hoppers
float low in the water, and that emerging midges hang vertical-
ly in the surface film.

In presenting a fly to the fish in a way that won't spook it,

I will assume that you have certain skills. And while you may not yet be able to toss a fly thirty feet and land it on the proverbial "pie plate" or throw a reach cast so that the belly the line always falls upstream, Silver Creek is just the type of place you're looking for when you want to develop these abilities. The placid current and abundance of casting room, makes Silver Creek the ideal place to improve your fly-casting ability. A few hours on the stream with a knowledgeable caster or guide is all it takes to improve basic rod handling skills.

Silver Creek fishing also offers other opportunities for you to develop skills that are essential to becoming a successful spring creek fly-fisher. These skills have little to do with physical dexterity, but instead involve your mental approach to fishing these slow, clear waters. The real key to successfully fishing Silver Creek is patience. Patience in your approach to the stream, patience in staying with a fish until you take it, and patience in being willing to take the time to understand what is happening in the stream that surrounds you.

To fish Silver Creek successfully you need to slow down, take the time to observe the interaction of insects and fish, and intrude as little as possible into the underwater haunts of the trout you are seeking. Learning to be sneaky is a skill like any other. When you can stand absolutely still and do nothing but watch the habits and peculiarities of an individual fish for fifteen minutes, you are well on your way to becoming a successful spring creek fisherman.

Meeting the Challenge:
The Evolution of a Silver Creek Fisherman

It is important to know that you will be going through a predictable progression as you fish Silver Creek. While there are no shortcuts as you move from one stage to the next, knowing what to expect will make it easier to cope with early frustrations. It will also bring a speedier realization that not every other fisherman on the stream is phenomenally better than you are. And most importantly, it will help you understand that catching the fish of Silver Creek may not actually be your ultimate goal at all. It is just possible that Silver Creek will offer you other pleasures you will treasure even more.

First Stage: The Emerger

Its easy to identify a novice fisherman on Silver Creek – he or she is the one standing in the middle of a hatch with mouth agape. As a newcomer, your first impression of the stream is that it's a fly fisherman's paradise. There is no need to search for a feeding fish because, when the hatch is on, trout are rising everywhere. This feeling of nirvana soon fades when you find you're unable to hook even a single fish.

Your first day on Silver Creek may lead you to make plans to hold a mini-garage sale: "Cheap – Rods, reels, and miscellaneous fly fishing equipment for sale – Seldom used to actually catch fish." Or you may simply make the decision to head back home for a life of following hatchery trucks, or you may opt to fish only for voracious bluegills, or you may decide to just hide in the closet and weep.

On the other hand, you may become enthralled with Silver Creek and the thrill of new found angling challenges. So you take the first step to becoming a good Silver Creek fisherman – you accept that a no- fish day on a stream brimming with rising fish is only verifiable proof that nothing comes easy here. In a world full of brag and boast, we finally have something that lives up to its notoriety. While it may take you awhile, you will eventually appreciate this stream's tough trout.

It's important to realize that very little goes right on Silver Creek at first. The difficulty usually starts with fly selection. Even if you're an experienced fisherman, you may never have had to give much thought to what pattern you were going to use. In fact, you may never have even had to portray a real insect on the end of your line. And although your bushy, fast-water patterns have fooled fish on other streams, on Silver Creek they're just grotesque lumps of tinsel and floss to be ignored.

It takes drifting your offering numerous times past a dozen open mouths, however, before you finally admit that your standard assortment of flies from home may be worthless. It becomes apparent that throwing tried and true patterns – deer hair Irresistables, heavily-hackled Humpies and gaudy Coachman Trudes – only makes Silver Creek trout react like creatures from hell were being pitched into the water.

It may take a few hours without a strike before it becomes apparent that an effective imitation for Silver Creek must usually be so realistic that, when floating next to a living insect, you can't tell your fly from the real thing. To obtain the exact duplicates needed, you have a choice of purchasing them at a well-stocked, fly-fishing shop, or tying them yourself.

Soon, you begin rejecting flies tied with a bunch of hackle fibers for a tail, in preference for flies where two or three microfibbets are used to duplicate a perfect mayfly tail. You quickly replace all of your thick, fat-bodied creations with flies where only a few twists of dubbing or hackle quill are used to produce a body having a much more realistic, thin profile. You now reject flies with wings made of thick hanks of hair in favor of flies with cut wings, Swiss straw or any of a half-dozen synthetic materials that give a better match to the translucent shine and shape of the real thing.

As your selection of flies improves, you gain confidence in their ability to catch fish. But you need to realize that this is only the first of many transformations needed to go from freestone to spring creek fishing. Your next step is to acquire equipment designed for this delicate, precise type of fishing. With the purchase of a 4- or 5-weight rod, the 6- weight rod is, except for special occasions, delegated to the closet. Then you may just have to get that 3- weight outfit. And now that 2 and 1-weight rods are available, you realize that these can often be the perfect spring-creek rod. Somehow, somewhere, sometime down the road, you'll be smitten and end up opening your wallet to obtain at least one of these ultra, light-weights. Using fisherman's logic, tell your spouse that if you buy the rod now you'll be able to get all those extra years of enjoyment out of it later.

The weight of the lines you are using also drops as the rods become lighter. Tippets get smaller. At first, you'll think it is impossible to bring in fish on monofilament as light as 6X –that's only 3.5-pound test. But once you're comfortable using 6X, you'll decide to give 7X – 2.5 pound test – a try. And then, carried away with your madness, you'll purchase your first spool of 8X.

But even as equipment improves, success doesn't come until your observation skills are honed and you have developed techniques to solve each new fly fishing problem. Early in your Silver Creek career, you'll have little understanding of the dynamics of this special stream. You may scatter your casts shotgun fashion over the surface in an attempt to find at least one fish dumb enough to strike. You will stereotype the fish as being finicky, finny animals that feed on everything but what you are imitating. At this stage, your goal is not to catch a lot of fish or big fish. It is to catch any fish.

As a newcomer to Silver Creek, you can let a few fishless experiences dent your ego and head for easier water, or you can accept the challenge, learn the insects, obtain the flies and develop your skills. There is only one guarantee on Silver Creek – if you keep at it, you will be rewarded with that first strike. That first trout will be one of the most memorable fish you ever take – now if you can just figure out how to land it on that 7X tippet!

Your first reaction to Silver Creek is very predictable – elation to embarrassment to depression. Hopefully, depression will be followed by determination and that will gradually bring you back to elation.

Second Stage: The Dun

There is only one way to reach this stage – by hanging in there. You read everything Harrop, Swisher, Richards, Whitlock, LaFontaine, Borger, Caucci and Nastassi, McCafferty, Schwiebert, Rosenbauer and others have to say on the subject of aquatic insects, trout, and fly fishing. Maybe you try Silver Creek with a guide so that you can at least learn the basics that would otherwise take several seasons to acquire. Most importantly, you stop treating your fishing experiences as hit or miss excursions and accept them as a series of lessons or opportunities that serve to build you into a spring-creek fisherman.

Slowly your approach to the challenge of fishing Silver Creek changes. Instead of viewing the stream as your nemesis, you begin to see it as a chance to get a doctorate in fly fishing. Here you observe improvise, test, scheme, devise and create. Silver Creek is a classroom.

Now you begin to appreciate all of those patterns you had

always considered fantasy designs by fly tiers who just wanted to get their name attached to a new fly pattern. Suddenly, parachutes, no-hackles, emergers, cripples, midges, floating nymphs and other recent creations are all solutions to specific fly- fishing challenges. You expand and refine your fly selection at the same time.

Although there is no reason you can't enjoy fishing with middle-of-the-road equipment, if you become a Silver Creek addict, you may search for solutions by upgrading your fly-fishing paraphernalia. You may buy the best. Although a top-of-the-line rod, reel and line are never a substitute for skill, they do make it possible to pitch a fly with a touch more power, throw more accurate casts, and play a fish on a more sensitive drag and finer tippet.

Most importantly, your observation skills begin to improve. Before you even enter the water, you take a long look at what is happening on the stream. Now, when one technique doesn't work, you change your fly, casting location, or presentation. Put simply, you don't flog the water for an hour with a dry fly when the fish are taking nymphs just below the surface.

As your appraisal, knowledge, and skills improve, you catch more and more fish. Your confidence grows until just any fish is no longer stimulating enough for you. Your challenge becomes "big" fish. Because the ability to become a big fish must certainly be accompanied by a large degree of intelligence, you assume the big fish to be a very "wise" fish.

You begin to explore new techniques. Since big flies take big fish, you start using hunky hoppers, fluttering damsels and ugly-looking leeches. You listen when other fishermen speak of the effectiveness of beadhead nymphs and you develop a sense of which new "fad" flies are worth trying and which are worthless before they even hit the water.

Soon, you start spending more time fishing where conditions make the likelihood of finding a big fish is highest. You twitch heavily-weighted flies through deep, dark, bottomless pits. You throw bug-eyed damsel nymphs to the long, black, distorted shadows cruising Sullivan Lake. You drift weighted nymphs through the deep channels of the S-bends. And, if you are more than a touch crazy, you tie up some huge mice out of caribou, antelope or deer hair and drag these monster flies over the water during the dark of night.

And while you know of the belief that huge flies take huge fish, you soon learn when just the opposite is true. You learn that mayfly hatches, too can get three, four and five pound fish up and feeding on the surface. This can happen during truly abundant hatches of brown drakes or Tricos. It happens in dead-still back waters where giant cruisers look for leftover Callibaetis spinners. And it can happen during even a light hatch of size 22 blue-winged olives when trout sense that the winter menu will be little more than appetizers – better a Baetis now than two midges later.

For some anglers meeting the challenge of Silver Creek is accomplished whenever a fish of twenty inches or better is taken. For others, there is one more level.

The Ultimate Stage: The Spinner

For those that reach it, the final stage in the evolution of a Silver Creek fisherman is different for every angler. For years I thought my ultimate goal should be to catch a thirty-inch fish or at least be able to take every fish that rose within casting distance. Now I know these goals only insure that most trips will be failures and that the only way never to be disappointed is to seek only to have a new experience every time I fish Silver Creek. I don't expect you to measure your own success by these same parameters, but I think you may come to some of the same realizations.

The first real insight I have had in trying to meet the challenge of Silver Creek is that fishing here can be pursued with an unbelievably simple approach or treated like a complex mystery where clues are gathered over a lifetime. A fisherman's personal philosophy on this is easily determined by taking a quick peek into his or her fly boxes.

An examination of my fly selection is a lesson in aquatic entomology. Every species of insect is well represented by an entire series of different ties. After tying the prototype for a particular insect, I constantly refine the fly. I continue to utilize the best features of each pattern, while dropping dozens of brilliant, but less-than-effective variations.

The adult damselfly is a great example of my quest for the perfect fly. My original tie imitated the long, segmented blue body with an extended body formed from blue-dyed deer hair. The flat, protruding wings were represented by the tips of creamy, white hackle. A grizzly hackle was wrapped around the body to make the fly float.

Subsequent patterns saw the body tied from rods of dense, blue foam rubber, a piece of old fly line, twisted forty-pound monofilament and a combination of yarn and tinsel. The opaque wings were replaced by strands of crystal poly yarn. These were more translucent than the feather wings but had a tendency to clump together. These wing balls gave way to thin films of plastic cut from a sandwich bag. But these were too noisy, too difficult to cast, and too phony to fool a fish. The flapping plastic was then changed to a pinch of calftail hair. Although the calftail was an improvement, it was a bit too opaque and bulky. The search for the perfect fly continued.

Today, the damsel I find most effective is tied with a twisted yarn body, wings made of strands of crystal organza, and a set of black, plastic eyes. Although still not perfect, I guess the fish take it for a damsel fly in distress, but even if they think its one of the God-awfulest, blue-bellied grasshoppers ever to have fallen into Silver Creek, all that matters is that they get the urge to attack my fly. Although I now have an imitation that works well, I have no doubt that five years down the road, I will be using a very different imitation in my attempt to fool even more trout.

So I have taken the complex route to solve the challenge of this stream. I will work toward developing the perfect fly for every possible condition. For me, the Silver Creek experience is a combination of entomological discoveries, strange new fly creations, and the constant alteration of approach and presentation. Scientifically, there is no way I can gauge the success of my strategy. As a fisherman, I have convinced myself it all works and I compliment myself for my skill and insight every time I catch a fish. When I don't catch fish, I often blame the fish!

You may well want to select a simpler route. Limit you fly selection to a few basic patterns you have confidence in and then use them until they produce. I might even envy you and your ability to reduced the sport to a point where it is little more than you and the trout. Often aficionados-of-the-minimum have had to put many years in on the stream to reduce their approach to flyfishing to its simplest form. To keep it simple, however, may first require you to work your way through the complex.

Some day, I may be fishing like the celebrities that take part in the fishing contest now held on the Snake River in eastern Idaho each year – the "One Fly Contest" or something like that. You pick out your favorite fly and then restrict yourself to using just that one pattern – a handicap that is intended to make the contest even more challenging. But while this restriction may make the fishing more interesting, it will be a long time before I feel the need to make fishing Silver Creek even more of a challenge.

Any fisherman can do well on Silver Creek when circumstances are perfect. The presence of a good hatch, a light chop on the water, periodic cloud cover, and hungry fish make it hard to fail. A slight variation of any of these factors, however, requires that your game plan be completely changed. It is at these times that all those years of observations pay off. Having an inherent knowledge of the stream means that you realize that when fish won't respond to the traditional Elk Hair Caddis imitation, a low- riding, Delta-wing Caddis pattern tied with hackle tips for wings may be eagerly accepted. It's sensing that when the stream is seemingly hatchless, there will always be a sparse hatch of pale morning duns coming off around a special section (just downstream of the headquarter building) of Silver Creek called the "Islands". It's the ability to look at fifty yards of seemingly identical bank and knowing that the fish will be holding two feet down from where a small shrub overhangs the water.

The fact that it may take years to absorb all of this information is tempered if you remember that you could live to be 200 years old and still never completely understand what is happening everyday on Silver Creek. All you can do is to learn enough to begin turning the odds in your favor. By taking pride in every new tidbit of information you enter into your flyfishing computer, every trip – even the less than spectacular ones –

begin to take on a value of their own. Sometimes, you even find more is learned on the off day that causes you to stretch, to explore and to try new techniques. You have come a long way as a Silver Creek fisherman, when someone asks "How's the fishing?" and you answer with a smile, "It's wonderful, the fish are nearly impossible to catch today!"

As your stockpile of fishing information grows, you may find that the need to catch lots of fish or to take "big" trout diminishes and is replaced with the overwhelming desire to take "that" trout. The definition of "that" trout being any fish that constantly refuses your offering and forces you to solve the mystery or fail. To me, the real challenge of fishing Silver Creek is in developing the ability to solve the fishing problems that are presented to you each day you are on the stream.

One of the best days I have had on Silver Creek took place on one of those days in late October where it's difficult to decide if its cold or warm. The air was dry with a hint of dust and everything seemed to be cloaked in a hue of golden orange. There wasn't another soul on the stream and I had that feeling of being the last person on earth.

As I entered Silver Creek, there was a very light hatch of blue-winged olives concentrated in the center of the stream. I tied on a simple parachute imitation wound around a wide-gaped, short-shanked, size 16 spider hook. I spent the next half-hour obtaining so many refusals that even a short strike would have been a big deal. Then the hatch petered out and the fish quit rising.

The end of the hatch left me standing in the middle of the stream with my head up my . . . well let's just say I had some time on my hands when I spotted a lone trout rising next to the bank-hugging cattails. He was picking off the last of the blue-winged olives as they passed by his position. He – the fish turned out to be an old male – never missed his target.

I started to cast to this fish and was soon repeating my previous performance of stringing together an unbelievable number of refusals. I changed flies to a size 20 parachute with a Swiss straw wing wrapped with a dun-colored hackle. I placed my offering more precisely. I tied on a lighter tippet. I tried to match the somewhat sporadic rise rhythm of the fish. I couldn't get a strike.

And then it happened. The perfect cast, the prefect drift, the perfect timing. Somehow, when the fly was still two feet from the trout, I sensed that this cast – one of a hundred – was the one that would bring him up. I was ready and when he sipped in my fly, I made the perfect lift and hooked him – yes perfectly – in the jaw just under the nose.

The fight was a good one. The rainbow launched itself three feet straight up, followed with a line wrenching run and a horizontal leap followed by several head shaking episodes. As I landed the eighteen-inch, red-sided rainbow, I took a good look at it and, as with every trout I catch, was amazed at its overwhelming beauty. I let the fish go.

I looked to see if anyone had seen my magnificent coup, but there was no one around. Then it dawned on me how fortunate I was to have this special place to myself. If I could have been anyone or anywhere, I would still choose to be me and I would be here – fishing Silver Creek.

On that day, I felt I had finally met the ultimate challenge of Silver Creek. Although I had always thought that the challenge was in catching the smartest, biggest, most selective trout, I have found the real challenge was finding contentment, the most elusive of all our desires. For the first time, I realized that the magnetism of Silver Creek is nothing more than its ability to make me happy.

Even though I had only fished for a couple of hours, I realized it wasn't going to get any better than this. Tomorrow, there would be new problems and new conquests, but today could only be perfect if I sank the point of my fly into the cork handle of my rod and went home. Bad day on Silver Creek? Never had one.

5
Having the Right Stuff

To enjoy the fishing at Silver Creek, you don't need to show up with gear to match every possible fishing situation you will encounter. You will soon realize that the use of the proper flies and leaders are necessary, but other paraphernalia allows for only minor refinements of fishing techniques. With a few small additions or slight modifications, the tackle you are now using on other streams will work well on Silver Creek.

If you have crossed the line, however, and have come to Silver Creek because it represents the ultimate challenge of your fly fishing ability, you will be looking for that edge that will allow you to elevate your skills to a higher level. Although you can present a weighted wooly bugger or midge emerger using the same leader, line and rod, the edge usually goes to the fisherman who selects a specific outfit for a specific situation. With equipment perfectly matched to each fishing situation, your chance of success and, maybe more importantly, your confidence of success greatly increases.

Rods

It's impossible to select an ideal rod for all the fishing conditions you will encounter on any given day at Silver Creek. During an early-morning Trico hatch, you might prefer to have a light-weight rod designed to cast short distances with a quick, flicking action. When the Tricos disappear with the first gentle breeze, you may want to switch to a slightly longer, medium-weight rod to pitch damselflies to those dark shadows at the edge of the weed patches. As the breeze grows into a full-blown blast that drives the damsels off the water, you may feel out-of-place without a gutsy, 6-weight rod for catapulting big hoppers into the wind. And if evening finds you in a float tube, the extra length of a nine or 9 1/2-foot rod makes it that much easier to get your line off of the water in preparation for your next cast.

Unless you can find a gillie to carry along this assortment of rods, you will need to choose one rod that will meet most of your needs or return to your vehicle several times during the day to swap fly rods. Either way, you still have the problem of selecting the right rod at the right time. To do this, your main considerations should always be wind speed, the type of fishing you expect to be doing, and the ability to achieve the best presentation possible. The lightest rod you would probably consider using on Silver Creek is a 2-weight (although I haven't had the opportunity yet to try the newer 1-weight rods). When these rods first came out, many fly fishermen saw them as nothing more than high-priced toys – wet noodles too light to cast into the wind and overmatched for any trout more than eight inches long.

I admit finding these lightweight rods underpowered on the cast myself until I switched from the recommended 2-weight, double-taper line, to a 3- weight, weight-forward line. The heavier line turns these rods into powerful mini-sticks that load quickly and can throw a line that penetrates winds of even moderate speeds. These wispy rods are perfect for the repetitive motion of cast-drift-cast-drift, have the ability to place line on the water with less impact than a fluffy milkweed seed, and the flexibility to keep tippets from breaking even when playing relatively large fish.

But although fishing these can be a delight, 2-weight rod days are rather limited. When afternoon winds pick up, or you want to tie on a weighted fly, or decide to throw long to bank feeders the lightweight outfit is nearly useless. Under these circumstances, or if you have made a vow to only go after fish of three pounds or better, a 4- or 5-weight rod provides the ideal combination of weight, power, and backbone the angler needs on Silver Creek.

Under certain conditions, a 6-weight or an even heavier rod may be your best choice. If you are purposely hunting large brown trout, you should consider yourself outmatched when using lighter gear. Night fishing with mice imitations or, if you're really serious, small muskrats – just kidding – requires "going loaded for bear." Fishing brown drake imitations, plopping hoppers along deep, dark undercut banks, and taking stonefly nymphs to the bottom of the deeper pools on Silver Creek are activities that will make you wish you had "gone with the big stuff."

The length of a rod can also make it possible to improve your presentation. Short rods of seven to 7 1/2 feet in length help to locate flies with precision, cast short distances into the wind, and don't cause fatigue. Long rods of eight-to nine feet in length are perfect for handling or mending line, allow you to get your line up high when your back is to a wall of cattails and supply more power for throwing large or heavy flies. Rods that are nine feet or more in length are perfect for float tube fishing.

Reels

Reels have two uses: to store line and to provide a controlled resistance or drag on fast-running fish. Any reel with a good, precision drag and the capacity to hold a line and seventy-five-yards of backing will do an excellent job on Silver Creek.

Because of your ability to adjust the drag to provide varying amounts of resistance, the smooth operating disk drag reel is the best choice for fishing on Silver Creek. Rim-control reels can be used, but if you don't apply tension evenly or if you catch your fingers in the fast- spinning handle, you can expect a break off when using light leaders.

Although it is nice to have the option of switching from one type or weight of fly line to another, this is not as necessary at Silver Creek as it may be on freestone rivers.

Backing

You never think much about backing until you hook your first twenty-inch Silver Creek rainbow. Then, if you have properly set up your reel, you will be treated to the beautiful sight of forty or fifty yards of line and backing heading downstream. No backing-no beautiful sight!

Since you usually only tie the knot used to connect the fly line and the backing once during the life of your line, it pays to do it right. The nail knot is widely used to make this connection and tied properly is a neat, dependable link between line and backing. If this small knot is well coated with head cement it will easily flow in and out of the guides and prevent a hang up that could loose a fish.

Line

The line of preference on Silver Creek is a floating line with a weight-forward taper. The moderately heavy touchdown of this line as it hits the water is a small trade off for being able to cast longer distances and into any wind.

Idaho is one of those places where, if the wind isn't blowing when you walk out of the house, you tend to pause and note this very special day in your diary. For most Silver Creek anglers, double-taper lines tend to have very long life spans – you just don't get much of a chance to use them.

Because of the abundance of plant life and the predominance of shallow water conditions, you seldom need a sinking line.

Since trout spook easily when a fly line passes over them,

you can assume that a brightly colored line in fluorescent orange or neon green will get them even more excited. You should consider using lines in neutral, earth-tone colors such as slate grey, olive or tan, but I admit to using the luminous hued lines without a noticeable difference.

Leaders and Tippets

The fly may be your single most important piece of equipment, but without the correct leader, flies are only worthless specks of fur and feathers. Today's very realistic fly patterns provide you with the edge you need to fool Silver Creek's wary trout. The phenomenal success of no-hackles, midges, emergers, and cripples is only possible because of the parallel development of super-strong, small-diameter leaders.

The role of a leader used at Silver Creek is the same as for any other stream; to come as close as possible to presenting a fly that looks as if it wasn't tied to a leader, a line, a reel and, ultimately, a fisherman. To understand how important leader performance is on Silver Creek, just toss a fly onto the stream with no leader attached. Then watch the fly float steadily at the exact same speed as the current. Achieving this uninhibited motion is your goal. Your fly will never drift as naturally as the real thing, but on Silver Creek, success is a measure of how close you can come to accomplishing the impossible.

Selecting the Proper Leader

Selecting the proper leader is your first real Silver Creek challenge. As with most Silver Creek problems, everything at first seems so complicated — but it really isn't. In priority order, you have five considerations when choosing a leader for use on Silver Creek:

- Choose a leader that will keep drag to a minimum.
- Choose a leader that will reduce drag even more.
- Choose a leader that won't spook the fish.
- Choose a leader that matches the size of your fly.
- Choose a leader that can handle the biggest fish you want to land.

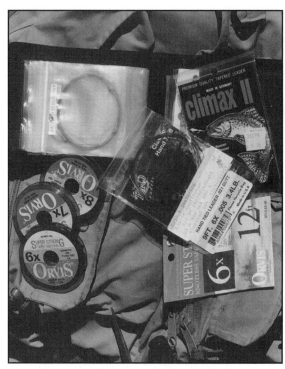

Leader selection can be critical when
fishing Silver Creek.

In choosing the correct tippet size, first look at the what the wind is doing. On one of those not-a-hint- of-a-breeze mornings the water looks like a giant mirror. Later in day, even the arrival of the lightest breeze causes thousands of tiny riffles to move across the surface of the water. The appearance of the afternoon winds cause a definite chop to form on the surface. If a thunderstorm or cold front follows with an all out blustery blow, you see waves that spray over the surface as they crest. With each increase in the speed of the wind, the distortion of the surface increases and it becomes more and more difficult for the trout to distinguish the profile of the leader or notice a dragging fly. When the water is dead calm, fish see and sense everything. In a full-blown November gale, you could use a winch and take fish.

After observing the wind, selection of a tippet size is easy. On a dead calm day, a fly tied on anything other than a 7X leader produces very little in the way of strikes. As soon as there is a breeze to rumple the water's surface, you can move to 6x for added strength. As the small ripples turn into mini- whitecaps, a 5X tippet will often be ignored by the fish. When water blows off the surface and hits you in the face, go home!

Now that a gossamer stand in size 8X has been developed you may be tempted to give it a try. While I can't deny that this finest of tippets may produce a few more strikes, I have found it is too weak to land the majority of fish hooked. The frustration of break off after break off (usually on the take) is just too great to justify its use on Silver Creek. Another important reason to avoid this lightweight tippet is the tendency you might have to play large fish into complete exhaustion in an attempt to land them.

Leader length tends to be a little less important. In most cases a nine-foot leader keeps the intimidating fly line an adequate distance away from the target fish. Occasionally – usually on days when the winds are calm – a twelve-foot leader seems necessary to pacify finicky trout.

Again, it may seem that the tackle manufactures have come to our rescue by providing fifteen-foot leaders that are, as they say, "Specially designed for use on spring creeks." But again, in an attempt to go beyond what is practical, these long, limp leaders are difficult to control which causes accuracy problems and are difficult to cast when there is even the slightest breeze.

After deciding on the size and length of the leader, your next consideration is whether to choose a hand- tied, knotted (compound) or a knotless (extruded) leader. The advantage of using a compound leader is that by varying the length of various sections as well as combining monifiliments of different hardness (stiffness) or softness (suppleness), you can obtain leaders that provide perfect turnover and accuracy under a variety of situations. Also, because you tend to throw tighter loops with knotted leaders, these cast much better than an extruded leader on windy days. The disadvantages of the knotted leader are it is more expensive or time consuming to buy or make and its knots have a reputation for becoming entangled in plant material. The knotless leader is less expensive and doesn't pick up plant fragments, but it is weak on accuracy and more difficult to throw into a wind.

On Silver Creek, the problem of plants adhering to knots is seldom faced because the vegetation is nearly always below the surface. A leader seldom comes in contact with the submerged vegetation and, since there is very little floating algae or scum, picking up plant debris is seldom a problem. When this is added to the fact that being able to hit a small target and cast into a stiff breeze are always important considerations on Silver Creek, the knotted leader tends to get the best marks.

I would have to admit that the knotless leader is the most commonly used type of leader at Silver Creek. But as a guide who has converted numerous clients to knotted leaders for the first time and watched how this type of leader instantly makes them into much better casters, I fail to see what (advertising? lower cost? availability?) has moved so many fishermen to use the knotless leader.

Asking anglers who are dedicated users of knotted leaders what their formula for producing a perfect leader would be, is like asking, "Who do you think should be the next President of the United States?" Everyone has a different opinion. Because of this and because I myself am constantly finding a new and improved combination that produces a better leader, I hesitate to make specific recommendations or give out formulas. I do suggest that you purchase a commercial compound leader and try it. If you feel the difference is worth a little extra effort then obtain a good book on the subject (consider getting several good books so you can compare all of the different opinions). Or even better, find someone who is an old-hand at this, and have them teach you how to tie your own leaders.

My current system to insure I always have the leaders I need for Silver Creek is to carry a large supply of 5X, 6X, and 7X leaders in nine- and twelve-foot lengths and several spools of 5X through 7X tippet material. With this combination of leaders and tippets, I find I have everything I need to quickly customize my leaders to match stream conditions. One other factor that influences selection of leaders is the size of the fly. A good rule of thumb states that the size of the tippet that is the best possible match for your fly can be determined by dividing the size of the hook by three. In other words, you would match a size 12 fly with a 4X tippet and a size 22 fly with a 7X tippet. In general, this is an excellent way to select a leader/tippet. On Silver Creek, this strategy is used whenever the trout agrees with your choice. If you can't entice the trout into striking, you can consider their vote as a firm "no."

The rejection of your offering increases greatly on those windless or near windless days when leaders look like a cowboy's rope to the fish. Regardless of what is considered proper leader choice under these circumstances, there is no choice other than to go with a finer tippet. There are many times when it will be necessary to attach a damsel fly on a size 12 hook to a 7X tippet in order to get a strike.

Casting large flies on fine tippet isn't easy and much of the time you will find that your leader hits the water in a pile, twists into horrible tangles, or misses your target by several feet. You can sometimes reduce these problems by using a shorter leader. Dropping from a twelve- or nine-foot leader to a 7 1/2-foot leader can greatly improve your ability to cast heavy flies on delicate tippets.

Only when you realize that the most important piece of equipment after the fly is your leader, do you give it its due. The same time and attention you give to tying, selecting, and preparing a fly, should also be given to insuring that you have on the leader that is going to best present that fly.

Landing Big Fish on Light Leaders

When contemplating the flat-water conditions often found on Silver Creek, it may seem there is little chance of ever using a leader strong enough to hold a good fish. Often this is true. If catching large fish is important, you should consider putting yourself into situations where super-light leaders aren't required! Fish areas where the surface of the water is naturally distorted such as along the edge where strong currents meet still water or other currents. Fish nymphs under the surface. Look for the opportunity to entice a trout to take a big hopper or other large fly. When put right on the nose of a large trout, these flies imitate half-a-days take of mayflies and can overcome a trout's natural wariness even when tied to bulky leaders.

But don't give up too quickly on the finer rated tippets. Today, 7X tippets are rated at a strength of 2.5 pounds. This may seem rather low if you are accustomed to using leaders with a better than five-pound breaking strength, but is still sufficient – if everything goes right – to land the largest fish now cruising Silver Creek.

If you have never used these finer leaders, getting a feel of just how much tension a tippet can withstand before it separates can be very helpful. To do this, try tying a series of 5, 6, and 7X leaders to your fly line. Then, one-after-the-other, tie the end of each leader to a fence post, tree or some stationary object. Now pull back on your fly rod and give each strand a good tug. You will be surprised by how much force it will take to break your leader. In fact, you may find yourself easing off on some of the leaders before they part because of a fear of breaking your rod.

With leaders costing more than three dollars each, this may seem like a very expensive lesson but, believe me, this experiment will give you great deal more confidence in the ability of lightweight leaders to handle heavy fish. It will also make you much more likely to use the spider web strands when conditions demand them.

Nymph Leaders

As with dry fly leaders, leaders for nymphing on Silver Creek are longer and leaner than those used on most streams. As a general rule, only floating leaders are used to present nymphs. A sinking leader simply gets your fly tangled in the vegetation.

This doesn't mean you won't sometimes sink your leader/tippet with some type of weight. It just means that under most conditions you will want to keep your leader on or near the surface while maintaining the option of strategically using weight to control the depth to which it, and the fly, sinks.

Typically, you start by matching your leader to the size of the nymph you are using – the heavier the fly, the heavier the leader. Your goal is to use as heavy a leader as you can, while getting as natural a drift as possible. If the fish won't hit, consider switching to a smaller tippet that has the flexibility you need. Since most nymphs used on Silver Creek are small – size 16 or 18 – the flexible 5 or 6X leader is most commonly used to obtain a nearly natural, subsurface drift. Since I find myself using 5, 6, or 7X leaders most of the time, I find it easy to switch off from dry fly to nymph fishing and back again, by just removing or adding a section or two of leader material.

Downright Heavy Leaders

Occasionally, you should head right for "winching" material. This may occur when fishing for the big, black shadow you have spotted just above a shallow, gravel bar, when flinging big flies within a few inches of deep, dark, undercut banks and, at night when listening to the music of brown trout slurping up anything that floats by that's smaller than a Canada goose.

Having discovered every possible way to lose trout on Silver Creek, we offer a few other tips for landing big fish:

• Rods with a lot of backbone are preferred when trying to land large fish, but power is secondary to finesse when using an ultra-light leader. With delicate tippets, using a rod with a soft or limber tip makes it possible to push a leader to its limits.

• Never fish with one of those little overhand knots in your tippet. It seems you always set your hook into the biggest fish of the day just after you have put a wind knot into the weakest section of your tippet and its strength has been reduced by forty percent or more.

• Avoid taking a strike when your leader has completely straightened out. Even a small fish can pop a tippet if they hit on a tight line.

• When setting the hook, the thought "strike" should never pass through your mind while at Silver Creek. "Lifting lightly" is a much better technique.

Waders

A good pair of chest-high, neoprene waders are perfect for the entire season on Silver Creek. When the water and weather are cold in the early spring and late fall, these waders keep you warm. They also provide warmth when float tubing where a lack of movement, the cool water, and a light breeze can combine to make you cold on even the warmest day. During the hot summer months, the spring-fed water of Silver Creek is still cool enough for you to enjoy the warmth the neoprene waders provide. Chest waders will allow you to wade nearly every inch of Silver Creek. Hip waders will allow you to get wet.

During the summer months, light-weight nylon waders are

also a good choice. You can extend the use of these waders during the cold weather by wearing long underwear, fleece pants, wool socks and a pair of neoprene booties. I have found this light-weight system keeps me warm well into October. After that, its neoprene or freeze.

Except for the lower stretch of Silver Creek, most of the stream bed is either silty, sucking mud, or coarse gravel. Rubberbottomed boots work very well in the mud and gravel of Silver Creek. Most fishermen, however, find the feltbottomed wading shoes they use on freestone rivers work just as well.

Shallow nets make it easier
to release fish unharmed.

Gravel guards are useful for keeping sand and pea-sized gravel out of your boots. Since water deep enough to have you standing on your tip toes while crossing the stream is commonplace, always wear a wading belt.

Clothing

Even when fishing Silver Creek in the summer, you will usually find yourself too cold rather than too hot. On a hot summer day, it is still a good idea to wear a long-sleeved, cotton shirt to break the wind, protect your arms from the sun's harmful rays, and to thwart the occasional mosquito attack. If the weather is questionable, a fleece jacket coupled with a light, nylon shell protects you from a cool wind or cold rain. When float tubing, a pair of fleece pants or insulating underwear helps slow the loss of body heat. Except for a rare summer thunderstorm, a good rain jacket is only needed on a frequent basis during the month of June.

In most other states, Idaho's early spring and late fall season would be called winter. During this time of the year, you may want to wear a wool shirt, down vest, a medium-weight nylon shell and a stocking cap. One other essential piece of gear is a pair of fingerless, wool or neoprene gloves. Without a pair of these, you may have to cut short your November fishing trip because of extreme numbness.

You also need a hat with a full brim. Besides giving you that dashing look, it keeps the sun out of your eyes and shades your ears and neck. A hat also makes it possible to fish in the rain while wearing glasses and keeps you from stopping a flying size 8, laser point, chemically sharpened hook with your ear. With practice, a hat also makes an excellent net for capturing insect specimens on the wing and can be used to fan away the swarms of mayflies attempting to land on your face.

Net

A net is not only recommended to enable you to land your fish, but also to allow you to release your fish unharmed. It's simply easier to land a good fish with a net. When a fish is quickly controlled, you handle it less and release it in a healthier condition.

If you are worried about tangling a fish in the net, the new, shallow-bottomed nets are a good alternative. For the shallow net, select one with an opening a size larger than a conventional net. Fish larger than sixteen inches tend to pop right out of the smaller-sized, shallow nets. Also, regardless of what type of net is used, it should be equipped with a cotton or Dacron bag rather than nylon to prevent from scraping away the trout's protective slime and scales.

Float Tubes

There are a few areas on Silver Creek where wadding is not practical because of deep water or a stream bed of "bottomless" silt. Fishing from a boat or raft is illegal on Silver Creek, thus the only way to fish these areas is with a float tube.

Only a few years ago, float tubes were nothing more than a truck inner tube with a few ropes and a canvas seat attached. Your choice today is limitless. Now you can contemplate the selection of an oversized tube, a tube with a back rest and an assortment of pockets capable of housing a mini-fly shop or an u-shaped tube advertised as the "easy entry"

model. You should select a tube based on whatever meets the majority of your fly fishing needs.

Since most of the float tube areas at Silver Creek are shallow, you don't need fins (although now that people are floating through the deep water of the s- curves, more anglers are using them in this area). Because of the thick mats of vegetation found in Silver Creek, it is much easier to push off the bottom with your boots than trying to paddle with a pair of fins.

One further accessory I would recommend for use with a float tube is a chest pack vest. This is much more usable than a standard vest and keeps your flies higher and dryer as well.

Odds and Ends in your Vest

A few other items you will want to bring:

• Some type of fly floatant. Everyone who fishes Silver

Creek has their own preference; liquid, gel, or spray all work well.

• A good set of mini-pliers allow you to bend down barbs and close split shot. If you usually use forceps for this purpose, remember that you may not be able to get the pinchers of these into the gap of a size 18 or smaller fly.

• Forceps (hemostats) for popping the fly out of the mouth of a fish you are releasing. The Ketchum Release is a new tool for removing hooks that also does an excellent job. It is especially useful on small fish that don't need to be revived and can be released without handling. Because it pushes the hook out, this tool also has the advantage of not crushing down on the fly like forceps.

• An insect repellent for mosquitoes.

• Clippers you can use for cutting leaders. A long or retractable lanyard will allow you to reach down to the water's surface to snip the leader attached to a deeply hooked fish.

• Sun block, lip balm, and polarized sun glasses for the intense sun of the high desert.

• Strike indicators. Your choice of style. I have tried them all including the newest fad – CDC tied to a hook shank – and find yarn or the pinch-on , adhesive type to work best..

• Water bottle. The best are those made for bicyclists so that you can open the spout with your teeth. That way you don't have to put your rod down to take a drink in mid-stream. In the arid environment of the sagebrush desert, you always need plenty of water. Holsters for these water bottles that thread onto your wading belt provides the most comfortable means of carrying drinking water.

• If you're inclined to eat lunch, you only have three choices; get something at the stores in Picabo or Gannett or bring your own.

So there you have the rundown on basic equipment. If you

only bring the outfit you have used to fish your home waters, it's like playing golf with just a driver, a wedge and a putter — it's possible, but not very practical. If you want to par the course, or in our case, catch a few more fish, adding a few specialty items will improve your performance.

There are many locations on Silver Creek where
a float tube is a necessity.

Silver Creek Reflections

**Aerial view of the section of Silver Creek managed by
The Nature Conservancy.**

Silver Creek in fall dress.

Point of Rocks

Lower Slough area

Landing a Silver Creek Rainbow.

Brown Trout

**Float tubers look out of place as they hike through the
sagebrush to a favorite fishing haunt.**

Fishing the Mahogany Dun hatch near Point of Rocks.

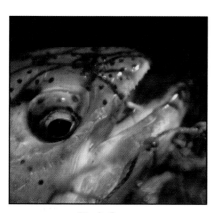

Rainbow

Wild roses

Silver Creek Rainbow

The "Preserve" visitor center.

A trout takes a mayfly.

Dave's Hopper

Poly Parachute

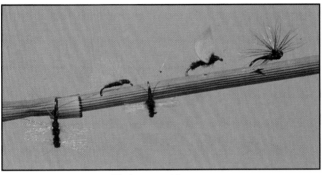

Trico patterns

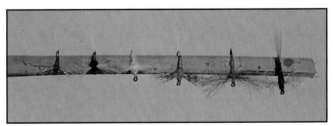

Spinner patterns

Quigley Cripple

No hackle

Black, red ants

CDC Trico

Caddis patterns

Damsel nymph

Damsel fly

Midge patterns

6
Flies and Ties

Before I became involved with fly fishing, I regarded bugs in one of two ways; if they could bite, they were to be avoided – if they couldn't, they were to be squashed. It was this sport that introduced me to entomology and to a fascinating part of my world that would have otherwise remained as obscure to me as Congress' thinking on how to pay off the national debt by giving everyone a tax break.

A real understanding of at least some of the complex behavior of these insects was to wait until I took a class in aquatic ecosystems held on Slough Creek, and the Lamar and Madison Rivers of Yellowstone National Park. I have spent the last decade doing my homework. It was fascinating. In the class, I found that caddis hatch by shooting themselves to the surface on a bubble of gas, mayflies have no mouth because eating is not necessary if your only goal is to mate, and the insect I once thought was some type of huge mosquito was called a crane fly.

When fishing Silver Creek, the understanding of insects and their unique life cycles is important to becoming a good fly fisherman and absolutely essential when it comes to selecting flies. What makes one hook covered in hair, feathers and plastic more effective than another is often a subtle distinction at best. Knowing what that subtle distinction might be is what selecting flies for spring creek fishing is all about.

Fly Selection: The Big Picture

If you prefer to purchase your files, developments within the last decade now make it easy to obtain an impressive variety of good-quality patterns. This is true even when you're looking for specialized flies that are only used on spring creeks. Fly shops and specialty catalogs now offer a wide variety of parachute, extended-body, emerger, no-hackle, and other patterns that weren't available fifteen years ago.

In most of these shops, fly patterns are designed to meet the conditions you will find on the local waters. But like buying a used car, you're the one responsible for making sure you'll be happy with your purchase. When choosing flies for Silver Creek, be finicky – small imperfections will be noticed by your quarry. Make sure the flies are the correct size and color. Check to see if the wing height, tail length, body shape, and hackle length all combine to create a well- balanced fly that will land on the water's surface with the wings pointed upward and not flop over like a capsized sailboat. Evaluate each fly on the quality of the materials used and the expertise of the tier.

In selecting flies, always consider how each pattern will imitate the living insect on the water and respond to current weather and stream conditions. For example, a traditionally tied Adams will work well as an imitation of a Callibaetis on a windy day, but when the winds are calm, it may take a parachute-tied pattern with a sparse hackle and perfectly formed cut-wing to fool the trout.

Be willing to experiment with all the various new patterns. Spinner imitations now come with wings made of hen-hackle tips, Antron, Z-lon, Cul-de- canard (CDC) feathers, clipped hackle, and various plastics. Viewed from underwater, each of these materials presents a slightly different image to the trout. Each fly also floats differently, has its own distinctive casting behavior, as well as a long list of other idiosyncrasies.

You should also feel free to modify existing patterns to meet your needs. Consider trimming the bottom of the hackle of a traditional dry fly to create a pattern that will ride low in the water. Or cut the upright wing off a pale morning dun parachute to create a perfect floating nymph.

Always be sure to have a few traditional and attractor flies in your fly box as well. In the past, these conspicuous patterns worked well on Silver Creek. Now, most spring creek fishermen feel the increase in fishing pressure has produced a well-educated quarry that consistently avoids these less than realistic flies. On the other hand, if most fishermen no longer use these flies, members of the most recent generation of trout may have lost their aversion to these "oddball" flies. True? False? All I know is that occasionally, when nothing else works, I tie on an attractor fly and, bang!

If you tie your own flies, select your patterns (or steal your ideas) from some of the more recent books that deal with the new wave of realistic fly patterns. Good sources include *The Dry Fly* by Gary LaFontaine, *Micropaterns: Tying and Fishing the Small Fly* by Darrel Martin, *Designing Trout Flies* by Gary Borger, *Mayflies, the Angler and the Trout* by Fred Arbona, and the recently published a *Tying Flie*s by Jack Dennis and Friends, and *Mastering the Spring Creeks* by John Shewey.

And, as far as spring-creek fishermen are concerned, *Selective Trout* and *Emergers* by Doug Swisher and Carl Richards are indispensable references. It is doubtful that any other works have had a bigger impact on the evolution of spring creek fishing than these two classics.

One other way to keep up with the most recent patterns and new developments in fly tying is to acquire some of the catalogs available on fly fishing equipment. The color plates displaying the flies sold by these companies are some of the best to be found anywhere and provide good guidelines for tying all of the current "hot" patterns.

Fly Selection: The Detailed Version

To many fly fishermen, the sometimes complex, sometimes difficult job of selecting flies may be too big a price to pay to become an effective spring-creek angler. They don't think the effort and hassle spent determining whether to fish a nymph, emerger, dun, spinner, or any of the in-between stages is worth it. But for many, this never-ending search for the perfect fly is what makes spring-creek fishing so special. It is this element of the sport that allows us a chance to use our brains, to be creative, and then, to get an instant evaluation by a worthy opponent.

To assist you in the pursuit of good, reliable patterns, you need to focus your efforts on imitating Silver Creek's "Big Five." These include five genera of mayflies: Callibaetis, Ephemerella, Tricorythodes, Baetis, and Paraleptophlebia. We couldn't resist mentioning the drakes – brown, green, and gray as well. During a season on Silver Creek, you will find yourself imitating these hatches more than any others. We discuss the body and wing colors for the nymphs, duns, and spinners, but this is an area you need to make your own decisions. Mayflies of the same genus often vary quite a bit colorwise. Some biologist have reported that color within the same species may vary with slight variations in temperature at the time of hatching. Another problem with selecting a color from a verbal recommendation or the text of a book is that individuals – especially writers – vary widely themselves as to what they would call a certain color; what one person calls brown another calls tan and still another calls it gray, etc.

Hook sizes are also included to provide the relative size of the insect. Sometimes more than one size is given because a genus may contain many similar insects that vary in size from one species to another. It is also possible for different generations of the same species of insect to vary in size.

Callibaetis – Speckled-Wings

Callibaetis or "speckled-wings" love slow water. Although these insects are found along the entire length of the upper portion of Silver Creek in The Nature Conservancy and Point of Rocks areas, they are most abundant in the sluggish water of Sullivan Lake, the Lower Slough, and the pond area above and below Kilpatrick bridge. The hatch of Callibaetis generally begins with the first warm weather in late June and becomes consistent by July. The hatch then continues into late September. The Callibaetis emergence is predictable, steady, and long lasting; it is the perfect hatch.

Experiencing a full-blown hatch and spinner fall of Callibaetis is something akin to scrapping the ink off of an Idaho lottery ticket and finding three $100 figures underneath.

Unfortunately, or maybe that's fortunately, I stumble onto more of these fantastic hatches than winning combinations on the scratch cards.

The best thing about the Callibaetis spinner fall and hatch is its predictability. It starts up in late morning as spinners begin their dance along the stream's edge. The distinctive, bouncy, up-and-down flight of the Callibaetis makes it easy to identify this insect even at a distance of thirty feet. As the day warms, spinners commence to lay their eggs. Coinciding with the spinner fall, a hatch of duns begins that may last for up to four hours. Some days the spinner fall is the greatest draw for fish and on others,

Poly Parachute

it is the hatch of duns. On the best days, both stages will get trout excited.

For whatever reason – perhaps temperature, or surface chop – this mayfly often seems to hatch in waves. Just when you think the hatch has ended, a new batch of mayflies appear and begin floating down the stream.

While many mayflies seem to love only overcast weather, the sun-worshiping behavior of the Callibaetis make them a favorite of anglers that often find themselves fishing on what seems to be an endless string of cloudless, summer days. On any bright day, a simultaneous outpouring of duns and egg-laying spinners is a near certainty around noon. An added bonus is that the Callibaetis also hatch when the sky is overcast.

Another big plus for the Callibaetis is that even if the spinners disappear when the afternoon westerlies start to blow, the duns will continue to hatch. This is one of the few hatches on Silver Creek that continues to emerge when the wind exceeds ten miles an hour.

Fishing during a Callibaetis hatch is just plain fun. During a heavy hatch, trout typically remain in one place and "have breakfast in bed." During lighter hatches, when the Callibaetis start to thin out at the end of an emergence, or on the ponds where there is no current, fish patrol large beats searching for tasty morsels. At these times, trout must feel like they are at a cocktail party where only hors d'oeuvres are being served. Anticipating only a bite here and a bite there, the fish make sure to grab as many cheese puffs and shrimp balls as possible.

The Poly Parachute and compara-dun in size 14-18 are both good Callibaetis patterns. A secret in tying a good dun imitation is to construct a fly with a much darker wing than what you perceive the natural to have. Although the dun has a mottled wing, the best flies seem to be those tied with solid colored, dark gray or black wings. In your hand, side-by-side with the real thing, the black-winged fake looks much too dark. On the water, you can't tell the darker fly from the natural.

Because exhausted spinners are often present on the water when the duns are hatching, the use of a spent-wing imitation should not be ignored. The spentwings have clear wings, but they are still mottled and a blend of light and dark (mostly light) materials may need to be used.

For continued success, I have often found it necessary to switch back and forth from imitating duns to spinners during a hatch. It seems some trout like their eggs sunny side up while others like them scrambled.

When you know that trout are keying on Callibaetis duns, don't hesitate to use nymphs if dry flies won't produce a strike. Even though the trout seem to be taking every dun in sight, the stomach contents of fish during this hatch indicate the trout's diet includes plenty of nymphs as well. Pitching a Gold Ribbed Hare's Ear, Gray Muskrat, or a Pheasant Tail nymph on a size 16 hook all seem to be acceptable imitations of the Callibaetis nymph which is a dark tan/brown.

Sparkle-duns, compara-duns, CDC emergers, and crippled stillborns are all types of imitations that can be effective Callibaetis copies

Ephemerella – Pale Morning Duns

The Pale Morning Dun or "PMD" is one of my favorite mayflies because of its beauty and, after the long winter, it is one of the first good hatches of the new fishing season. After leading the way in June, PMDs hatch fairly consistently through the entire summer. A large species of PMD, infrequens (size 14/16), is present in early summer to be joined by the smaller species, inermis (size 18/20) in late June and early July.

Pale Morning Duns, as their name implies, often appear in the morning. On Silver Creek, however, it is usually only the spinners that show up early in the day. Duns shy away from the intense sunlight of early mornings and cloudless afternoons and often only hatch in the low light of dusk. The exception of this would be cloudy, rainy, or overcast days when heavy hatches often appear.

Poly Wing Spinner

In the evenings with the sun low in the sky, good emergences of PMD's are the reward for the angler willing to stay out until twilight. Quite often the hatch will increase in intensity during the last thirty minutes of daylight. During this period, trout are less finicky and fly patterns are not as critical. I have had great success with size 16 Parachute Adams, which are not at all close to the color of the naturals and leads me to believe that the size, silhouette, and presentation are the key at dusk.

It is common to see good PMD spinner falls in late July and August mixed in with the Trico spinner fall. While more trout seem to select for the more abundant Trico, individual fish may be seen inhaling the larger PMD spinners as well. Fishing a large, light colored PMD spinner instead of a tiny, dark Trico imitation can be much more of a pleasure if you don't have the eyes of a hawk. Simple Poly-wing Spinners do a good job of matching PMD spinners. A spinner pattern using Swiss straw for wings also seems to work very well at the end of a hatch when trout are cruising for "leftovers."

The pale white/gray wings and light yellow/olive body of the PMD dun make it an easily identifiable mayfly and a wide variety of imitations are available. On windy days, a Yellow Humpy (an attractor pattern) and the Light Cahill (a traditional pattern) work well. When the wind is calm, more realistic ties like no-hackles, parachutes, or compara-duns often fool discriminating fish. PMD hatches fade quickly as September arrives.

Struggling nymphs and stillborns are common with the PMD and good emerging patterns for the PMD are floating nymphs, CDC emergers, cripples, or a sparkle dun. These flies are tied to represent mayflies as they are splitting out of their nymphal shucks in the surface film or ones that are unfolding their wings. They also imitate a mayfly which is unable to completely free itself of its nymphal shuck. To the trout, these patterns represent a mayfly at its most vulnerable. PMD nymphs vary in color from brown to dark brown.

Brown (Ephemera), Green (Drunella), and Gray (Siphlonurus) Drakes

Brown Drake

Of these monster-big mayflies, the brown drake is by far the more famous on Silver Creek. But since we discuss the magic of a full-blown hatch of this special mayfly later, we will concentrate on the more limited hatches of green and gray drakes. Although these two giant mayflies do not hatch in great numbers on Silver Creek, there numbers are great enough to get the trout and angler excited on certain days. The greens hatch sporadically in early June and the grays hatch from late June to early July.

Hatches of these drakes both last for about two weeks. These mayflies are seen on the water from late morning to mid-afternoon. Useful patterns include a large Parachute Adams or extended body flies in sizes from 10 to 12. These mayflies are found in The Nature Conservancy and through the Double RR Ranch, but are not seen in areas farther downstream.

Tricorythodes – Tricos

Like burning buildings and freeway smashups, Tricorythodes or "Trico" (also called White-Wing Blacks) spinner falls attract an unusual cast of characters. Perhaps it is a heart surgeon who fishes with the same exactness he or she uses when pushing a catheter through an artery. Or maybe it is a philosopher who loves to fly fish because the repetitive motion makes meditating easy. Or the good Catholic who occasionally skips church on Sunday because he knows God understands the pure joy of a water-blanketing fall of Trico spinners. And finally, there is the newcomer, the angler who giggles in excitement when he first sees a hundred sucking mouths within casting distance and ends up whining silently to himself when, three hours later, he haven't been able to hook a single fish.

What makes fishing the Trico spinner fall so difficult? First, even if the trout thinks your fly is a perfect match, the fly has to compete with thousands of the real thing. There's also the fact that even if a fish does take your offering, it will be nearly impossible for you to tell the fish has selected your fly out of all the other small black specks floating down the creek. Under these circumstances, the only way to hook a fish is to set the hook whenever there is even a remote chance that it was your fly that the trout just nailed. Then there's that feeding rhythm the trout get into as they rise like robots with built-in metronomes. You must be able to slide your fly into the mouth of a fish that is open for approximately one second out of every five. Getting your fly in place just as the fish rises is easy; all you need is the combined talents of an expert mathematician, a good wing shooter, and a genuine psychic.

Finally, there's that minuscule margin of error you are allowed when trying to drift a fly into your target. Let's see, a trout's mouth is about 1 1/2 inches wide. With the current funneling a long line of Tricos into every trout's mouth, the fish aren't about to move even an inch to take in an errant fly. Your choice is to put your fly into that eye of the needle or to clip it off, break down your rod, and head for another stream.

Trico fishing is a bit like trying to thread your tippet through the eye a size 28 fly while holding it behind your back. You know it can be done, but are you the one who can do it? But give up on Tricos? Not hardly! This is what Silver Creek fishing is all about.

Trico duns, at least the males, hatch in the late evening and usually end up as part of the nearly unidentifiable soup mix of bugs that are active just as the sun sets. In the early morning, the female duns hatch and quickly turn into spinners. The males then join the females flying in thin, swirling clouds at streamside. At this critical point, often on Silver Creek between 8 a.m. and 9 a.m., the mayflies either get blown completely

Trico Double

away by the wind or they mate and begin to drop to the water's surface.

When the horde of spinners lands, there may still be nymphs, emergers, and duns in the water. Some flycasters like to imitate these other stages, but I usually stay with the spinner and feel that presentation and persistence are more important than which stage I am imitating. The spinner fall often only lasts for an hour or so, but occasionally may extend well past the lunch hour.

Some people dream of finding a cure for cancer, being the first human on Mars, or developing an automobile that will run on water. My quest is even more difficult – to develop the perfect Trico spinner pattern. For wings, I have tried cut feathers, poly fibers, hackle tips, loops of monofilament, cellophane, strands of mylar, and micro web. I have even contemplated catching house flies (somehow using the wings of the Tricos themselves seems a little unethical), pulling their wings off and tying these to my hook. Humane Society aside, only my worry about being accused of using bait keeps me from trying it!

Trico patterns for spinners and duns are generally tied in sizes 18-24. Whatever pattern is used the distinctive narrow abdomen, bulky thorax profile and the relatively long set of three tails should be imitated. Imitations of the duns have olive bodies and white wings, while spinners patterns have olive and black bodies and clear wings and three very long tails. Nymphs are olive to dark brown.

For bodies, I've dubbed with poly, beaver, muskrat, otter, rabbit, hackle stems and just plain thread. To imitate the three long, white tails, I've tied on micro- fibbets, brush bristles, hackle fibers, moose mane, mountain goat hair, and Cul-de-Canard feathers. The end result has been a long parade of flies that have achieved the remarkable endorsement, "once in awhile they seem to work." With a new pattern always just over the horizon, this week's favorite Trico spinner imitation uses several 3/4-inch white micro-fibbets for tails, a thread body with a bit of beaver dubbing to form the thorax, and a bunch of fibers picked out of a sheet of organza and tied spent- wing fashion.

Tricos love the warmest weather Silver Creek has to offer and so are most persistent from mid-July to early September.

Baetis – Blue-Winged Olives

How many mayflies does a trout consume in a season? 1,000? 2,000? 20,000? I have no idea, but I do know that a very large percentage of these mayflies are of the species known as Baetis or, as most fishermen call them, "blue-winged olives." This common name has come to represent a large number of similar species in the genera of Baetis. In terms of total numbers, this genera of mayflies make up the most prolific hatches and spinner falls occurring on Silver Creek.

As with most areas, Baetis hatch on Silver Creek every month of the fishing season. A prominent hatch during the pleasant summer months, Baetis are often the only mayflies emerging during the cool, or even downright cold months of June, October and November.

Fall fishing during the blue-winged olive hatches is a different experience for Silver Creek devotees. Now the pace has slowed on the stream. Most of the fishermen and glamorous hatches are gone. But for some strange reason, even though a hundred of these small mayflies wouldn't make a good mouthful, big fish happily, and sometimes aggressively, continue to feed on these tiny bugs. For those who love briskly cold mornings that warm to sweater weather by noon, the hatches of blue-winged olives are but a another bonus during an already delightful experience.

On a recent October day, in the Point of Rocks area of Silver Creek, the Baetis hatch began in typical fashion. The hatch of olives begins as the day warmed into the low forties by midmorning. Smaller fish, with their typical splashy riseforms, were the first to take advantage of brunch but within an hour, the larger fish joined in. Easily spotted as they surfaced in delicate sipping rises that created small bull's-eye patterns on the water, these were the big- bellied fish I had come looking for.

Near the bank, I began watching a fish that seemed to have a particularly large gap between the dorsal fin and tip of the tail that occasionally pierced the surface. The trout's back and fins were so dark, I knew it was a rainbow and not one of the large browns where the color would be more that of a pumpkin. Absorbed in picking off blue-winged olives within inches of the yellow-brown grass of the bank, the rainbow was totally unaware of my presence.

After presenting several blue-winged olive dry fly patterns to the trout with no noticeable response, I decided a nymph presented just below the surface might be the solution. On my first cast, I tossed a size 18 Pheasant Tail nymph and yarn strike indicator a little too far and the rig became tangled in the grass. I pulled and the fly plopped into the water less than a foot from the bank. I watched as the strike indicator floated four feet to where I had last seen the fish. The tuft of yarn sank below the surface. After a second or two of hesitation – somehow I always assume I have hooked into a plant rather than a fish – I gave the line a gentle tug.

The fish erupted in a jump that came close to landing it on the bank. It was during this surge of energy that I noticed a loop of my fly line had wound itself around the reel handle and had effectively turned my drag into an anchor. Similar mistakes had cost me several good fish in past years, but for some reason, this time the tippet stayed intact through the jump and landing.

The fish made several long runs and cleared the water two more times. With the demise of much of the vegetation during this time of the year, I had little fear of the fish burying itself in the plants.

Three or four minutes later, I lead the fish into my net. I didn't have a measuring tape, but knew that the opening of my net is exactly nineteen inches. The fish was a good three inches larger than the opening.

Even though I felt a sense of urgency to return the fish to

the water as quickly as possible, I decided to check the contents of the its stomach. I slipped the hook out of the tip of the trout's nose and left the fish suspended in the pool of water within my net. I found my stomach pump, squirted in a stream of water and then siphoned everything out. The results were several blue-winged olive duns, a dozen or more small brown nymphs and one much larger nymph, probably a mahogany dun. For me, the experience proved once again that nymphs are often the best answer.

For the advanced angler, the blue-winged olive hatch offers plenty of opportunities to play detective and decipher exactly what approach will take the most fish – or any fish. At any given time, emergers, duns or spinners may be on the water at the same time. Tied with cut, CDC, poly, or calfhair wings, a dubbed body and monofilament, hackle or moose hair tails, an infinite variety of imitations of the blue-winged olive can be concocted. Sometimes, a few strands of Z-lon used to represent a mayflies' trailing shuck produces better results than tying on a traditional tail. Sometimes, a sprig of poly tied as a short wing to imitate the emerging dun will produce good results. And sometimes, a fly that doesn't resemble much of anything works best. For example, a Griffith's Gnat in sizes as small as size 24 is often taken greedily during a blue-winged olive hatch while those perfect mayflies with beautiful, upright wings bring only short strikes. It maybe that the gnat has a profile similar to a blue-winged olive emerger or that it resembles a the midges that are often intermixed in these hatches.

The Baetis are present on Silver Creek during the entire fishing season from May to November. Blue- winged olives are tied in sizes 18-24. Baetis duns have olive/brown/ bodies and dark dun-gray wings (hence the name blue-winged) while the spinners have clear wings. Nymphs are also olive/brown.

Paraleptophlebia – Mahogany Duns

Mahogany duns are just one more delight for the fall fisherman. Dispelling the notion that the larger the mayfly the earlier it hatches, the mahogany dun is copied by a size 14 to 16 fly with a dark, chocolate- brown body and slate gray wings. Mahogany duns emerge at mid-day in just-as-the-pumpkins-ripen fall hatches occur from early September to early November – and their presence never goes unnoticed by the trout. Found in Silver Creek from the headwaters to Picabo, fishing the dime-sized dun provides a nice relief for eyes that have been trying to spot a size-24, blue-winged olive fly all morning long.

A traditional tie that copies the mahogany dun is the Quill Gordon. A no-hackle or a Poly Parachute with dark brown or black wings are also good imitations. Another consideration is the use of a cripple or stillborn-fly pattern to imitate a mayfly that has become caught within its nymphal shuck during emergence. Tied in a 50/50 fashion (1/2 nymph, 1/2 dry fly), the Quigley Cripple is one of the best of these designs that I have found. The Quigley Cripple is a complex pattern with a marabou tail, a dubbed thorax, a deer hair wing and a grizzly hackle. The short segment of marabou is substituted for the standard hackle or hair tail to create the illusion of a trailing nymphal shuck. To the fly fisherman, the Quigley Cripple looks like a fly that was finished off by throwing it into a food blender set on fast chop. To the trout, the fly looks like an insect in distress.

Nymphs fished near the surface are also an effective technique of taking trout during a mahogany dun hatch. Nymphs are dark brown in color.

I once heard someone say that their aged father's sole reason for living was so that he could go bird hunting for a one month period in the fall. I know how he must feel. And when my own October finally rolls around and I can no longer wade in mud, stand for hours in freezing water, or fish the mahogany dun hatch, I hope my family will at least prop me up on the bank and let me watch a good angler cast to the last good hatch of the year. Somehow what comes last is always the most precious.

Trichoptera – Caddis

The best caddis hatches take place in the evenings during the warmest months of summer. Typically, this occurs in July and August when the afternoon temperatures rise into the high 80's. The one exception would be the inch-long October or fall caddis that hatches in September and early October after the summer heat has dissipated. Although sometimes present in the early morning and late afternoon, the best caddis hatches almost always take place as the sun begins to set.

Biologists have identified at least eighteen different genera of these insects at Silver Creek. I, on the other hand, have identified big ones, small ones, black ones and brown ones. I know an "expert" ought to know each species on an intimate basis, but sometime every time I ran into a good caddis hatch I reached for a fly rod instead of a entomology reference.

Delta Wing Caddis

Humor aside, I think the next twenty years of my life will be spent learning more about the lifestyles and importance of the caddis on Silver Creek. Most fishermen I have meet on the stream have only limited experience in fishing this hatch and most will do anything to fish mayflies instead. But having found that delta-wing caddis patterns are often much more effective than traditional, folded wing patterns, that drifting caddis pupae can produce good results when fished just under the surface like a nymph, and that the new plastic "bubbles" used to tie patterns that imitate caddis pupae that shoot to the surface on a gas bubble is fun to tie and use, my interest has been piqued.

Suffice it to say that the majority of the caddis at Silver Creek are in the 14-18 hook size category. There are also a good number of micro-caddis in the 20-22 hook-size and a few straw-colored giants in the fall that are in the 10-12 hook-size.

The Delta-wing Caddis fly pattern may be the single best dry imitation available, but realistic caddis ties, like the Henryville or the Harrops Slow Water Caddis are often very productive on Silver Creek because of their low riding characteristics. The higher floating, more visible elk hair caddis, however, is often the fly of choice for fishing into the evening darkness. The Elk Hair Caddis will also take a good amount of skittering or twitching without sinking. This is critical when you are casting a caddis fly downstream and then letting it swing.

This imitates the motion of a living caddis fluttering across the surface of the water.

Underwater, a variety of caddis larva and pupa, especially the Sparkle, Soft Hackle, and Peeking Caddis work well when caddis are emerging. Using a dead drift or a Leisenring lift sometimes provokes a trout into striking, but presenting the fly just under the surface often results in more strikes.

Stoneflies – Plecoptera

Stoneflies are most abundant in locations where the stream's bottom consists of gravel and where the current is at its peak. This requirement greatly limits the distribution of stoneflies on often silt-bottomed Silver Creek.

Yellow Sally

The large, orange and black stonefly of the west, the salmonfly (Pternarcys californica), hatches out on lower Silver Creek and on the Little Wood River. This stonefly hatches in the spring as soon as the water starts to warm, which typically occurs before the fishing season opens on Silver Creek and while high water still predominates on the Little Wood River. Because of this, fishing imitations of the adult stonefly is limited.

The large black stonefly nymph is about the only insect worth imitating on the Little Wood River in the early spring and this fly can take good fish on the lower section of Silver Creek during the entire year. Typical stonefly patterns incorporate mohair, dubbing, dental floss, chenille and rubber legs into an big, black fly where ugliness is a plus.

Smaller stoneflies – genera Isogenus – known as "little yellow Sallies" are found in upper Silver Creek. Most of these insects hatch in June and July. Nowhere near as abundant as mayflies and caddis, these hatches are still an important source of food to the trout. A good imitation is the high floating Stimulator with its orange head, yellow body, and hair wing in size 14 or 16.

Midges – Chironomidae

Midges are tiny runts of insects that could probably be christened with even the more common names than mayflies – the pale morning midge, the blue-winged olive midge, black-eyed midge and the itty-bitty midge. But no fly fisherman I know breaks midges down into as much as two groups. A midge is a midge is a midge.

Midge hatches occur year-round on Silver Creek, but not in the large numbers that are found on New Mexico's San Juan or Utah's Green River. On Silver Creek, midges occur as individuals and not in the nickel-size clusters found on some western streams. But to the trout, they are just like popcorn – if you eat enough, you eventually get full. When a stomach pump is put into the gullet of a fish feeding on midges, its not unusual to syphon up thirty or forty midge pupa and adults on just one squeeze. On the cooler days of spring and fall, these can often be the only insect emerging.

This hatch may pass unnoticed because it's nearly impossible to see midges on the water. In fact, it is often the persistent rise of fish to an unseen prey that serves as the best indicator that a midge hatch is taking place. When this phenomenon is coupled with the sight of mating swarms of adult midges near the edge of the stream – midges often mate immediately after emergence – you can allow blind faith to take over and just assume that a midge hatch is occurring.

On Silver Creek, trout greedily feed on midges in all stages of development. First, the threadlike pupa is gulped down as it rises to the surface or as it hangs in the surface film just prior to emergence. Then, after exiting the pupal skin, the adult midges are easy prey as they ride the current until their wings are ready for flight. Finally, the adult females are again susceptible to trout when they return to the stream to lay their eggs. Of all of these stages, the midge is most vulnerable as a pupa hanging in the surface film. The use of a stomach pump indicates that a dozen pupa are taken for every adult insect.

Three flies that require very different presentations seem to work well as midge imitations. On the surface, a Griffith's Gnat tied with only a few wraps of peacock herl with a single black or grizzly hackle wound through it is often well received by the trout. Mr. Griffith didn't design a very complex fly, but they did name this one for him and, in sizes 18 to 24, these can often be deadly. I've had good success with these same flies during Baetis hatches, so I'm not always convinced that the fish think they are midges, but I don't care what the fish is thinking as long as it takes the fly.

A good in-between fly is a simple emerger like the new Palomino Midge. Tied with nothing more than micro-chenille and a puff of white poly yarn, this fly can be tied in size 18 to infinity. In the water, the poly yarn floats on the surface while the body hangs into the water. The Serendipity tied with a Z-lon body and a deer hair head is another excellent pattern for imitating emerging midges.

Finally, the pupal or underwater stage of the midge can be imitated by any head and body tie in sizes 20 to 24. A good imitation seems to be nothing more than a underbody of green thread, a body of the latest plastic phenomenon – clear, midge lace – and a head constructed out of a single strand of peacock herl. When fished with a greased line (fly floatant applied to the tippet above the fly) and dropped a foot or two above a feeding fish, this can be a very deadly fly. The shallow nymph on a strike indicator techniques can also be very effective

Odonata – Damsel Flies

It's easy to identify a damsel fly fisherman – just listen. You can hear the fluttering sound the fly makes as it is propelled through the air, the distinct plop of the fly hitting the water, and the laughter and hoots of other fly fisherman. But it's going to take more than a few gaffs to get me to pass up the use of a fly that big fish find so hard to ignore.

I first discovered damsel fishing after a dismal day of casting over the mayfly hatch. I had just about given up and decided my best strategy might be to plop myself down on the bank and have a bite of lunch. With no fish rising, there wasn't much to watch – it was just hot, dead time.

Then, in the middle of the stream, a splashy rise caught my attention. I sat back and watched. The fish continued to rise sporadically, but never in the same location. The only predictable pattern I observed was that the trout always rose at the edge of the floating plants in the center of the stream. At the time, the only insects in the area were small groups of damselflies that were perched on these islands of vegetation.

Guessing that the trout might be feeding on the damsels, I pulled out of my fly box one of the largest flies I had ever used on Silver Creek – a size 12 damsel with a blue, deerhair extended body, cream- white feathers for wings and finished off with a grizzly hackle.

I cast the fly up next to the weeds. The fly floated for six inches and was taken in a tremendous swirl. I missed the fish and cast again. Within a foot of the first rise, another fish smacked the damsel. This one stayed on longer, but was soon lost to the weeds.

I soon realized that I wasn't

Damsel Fly adult

fishing to a single trout but to an entire school of fish. I missed two more strikes before my only damsel fly disintegrated. There was nothing else I could do but sit and watch the fish work.

The fish were like wolves working a small herd of caribou. When in a moment of mating rapture, one of the damsels would flop onto the water, a trout would move in and grab it. I also observed rises where trout came up through the edge of the plants scooping up both alga and damsels in the same mouthful, looking much like a submarine rising through the Arctic ice. I also saw trout swirl so violently just below the surface that damsels perched on the floating plant would be knocked into the water. Waiting jaws were always ready to end the distress of any floundering damsels.

Good damsel fishing depends on several specific conditions. First, it must be July or August when damsels are present in large numbers. It is also important that the adults be actively mating. This typically takes place in the mid-afternoon, the hottest part of the day. During this time, males chase females and their flamboyant mating style causes many of these insects to end up floating exhausted on the water surface. Finally, the wind cannot be strong but a slight breeze is great. A light breeze knocks damsels into the water and makes them fish food, a strong wind drives the damsels into the stream bank vegetation and away from the water.

Damsel Fly nymph

The beauty of damsel fishing is that it fills the void, the void being the doggy, slow-fishing time between the morning and evening hatches. When fishing damsels, your best results will come when covering lots of water. I usually cast, wait for the drift, take three steps forward and cast again. I can move quickly along the stream only because most other fishermen spend this time of day eating sandwiches and drinking a beer.

Cast at the bank and between the weed beds and concentrate on the edges of the patches of vegetation where the damsels are most active. This is not "fish after fish" action, but in a period of several hours I expect to get at least a few spectacular strikes and hopefully take at least one good fish.

Use your wildest imagination when tying damsels. There are many patterns and they all seem to work equally well. Unfortunately, some work equally bad too. I have tired many different materials to imitate the long rod of a body (blue for males, tan for females) and its transparent wings. I have several favorite patterns, but every season finds me with a new prototype. Make up your own version and have fun.

I have often taken trout by stripping damsel nymphs around the patches of vegetation. Experts say to always strip toward the bank since this is the direction damsel nymphs move as they hatch. This may be so, but it is impossible to fish across the weed beds of Silver Creek. Here fishing is mostly limited to the deep water channels between the plants, but pulling a damsel nymph weighted with a set of bug- eyes on the front upstream will often induce a strike.

I prefer a damsel nymph tied with black, weighted (for deep slots) or plastic (for shallow water) bug- eyes and olive/brown marabou for the thorax, abdomen and tail. Unweighted, these flies sink very slowly and can be maneuvered just above the plants growing on the bottom.

Grasshoppers

God either made hoppers because of a love for fish or fishermen.

Consider it. Why else, but for the benefit of the fish, would God build an insect like this one — big and bulky with incredibly powerful legs and a set of huge, batlike wings. This insect launches itself blindly into the air like a Scud missile with no specific target in mind. The hopper's wings resemble those odd contraptions that men first strapped to their arms in the feeble, often painful, first attempts to fly. Combined, these physical attributes turn the touchdown of every hopper into a crash landing. If the hopper hits land, it picks itself up and tries again. If it hits water, splat – it's fish food – a day's worth of protein packaged to be taken in a single bite.

Dave's Hopper

Or on the other hand, maybe it was the fly fisherman that God wanted to make happy. Here is an insect that draws fish like free money draws a crowd. The hopper is relatively easy to tie and it takes fish on the sloppiest of presentations. Either way, we should all be thankful for grasshoppers. On the lower, warmer, drier section of Silver Creek, I have seen grasshoppers so thick that every step taken along the bank would launch half-a-dozen of these bug-eyed insects into their spastic flights. Those that hit the water might float ten or twenty feet, but almost never further, before a trout rose to slurp it down. During these heavy hopper infestations – they occur about once every ten years – brown trout of every size fed near banks waiting for their next easy meal.

At the Bureau of Land Management access on lower Silver Creek, I can remember one particular nineteen-inch brown trout that rose to take a Joe's hopper with all the speed of a serious diner at an all-you-can-eat restaurant. When hooked, the brown seemed to be in a trance. Upon landing the semi-limp fish, the reason for such a response was obvious; the fish had a stomach the size of a lemon. The stomach was stretched so tight that you could feel the hoppers inside. I had hooked a couch potato complete with beer – no – hopper belly.

On the upper section of Silver Creek, I see hoppers most years during the period from July to September. By late summer of nearly every year, there are nearly always enough of these bugs around for the trout to recognize them.

One warm September, I remember fishing the upstream end of a deep pool shaped like a large horseshoe. There wasn't much activity until I noticed the nose, back and tail of a small fish roll up onto the surface near the far bank. I placed a Dave's Hopper about three feet above the trout's location and the current carried the fly on a perfect line. A trout rose out of the black water, but this fish wasn't the midget of thirty seconds earlier. Just the head and jaw of this trout was bigger than the first riser.

As with most large fish, the rise and subsequent slide below the surface seemed to occur in slow motion. It amazed me that so many things could run through my mind between the take and the strike. What size tippet do I have on? Did I tie just a clinch knot not or was it an improved clinch? Is he going to run up into that dead tree or down into the rapids? Is this really happening or is all of this just wishful thinking? Regardless of the answer to all of these questions, everything went perfectly.

The big brown dropped to the bottom of the pool and tugged hard. One exciting run covered more than thirty yards, but finished in the same place where it started. After several minutes, the fish relaxed and quickly came to the surface. The twenty-six-eight pounds or more. On most streams, the plop cast – smacking the water with a hopper fly to produce a purposeful kerplunk! – is the most popular technique used. On Silver Creek, the sound and vibrations this method produces often stimulate trout into streaking three feet or more to smack a hopper. But a drawback to using this technique is the tendency of Silver Creek trout to hold very near the water surface where the landing of a hopper bomb will often startle your target into

SILVER CREEK HATCHES

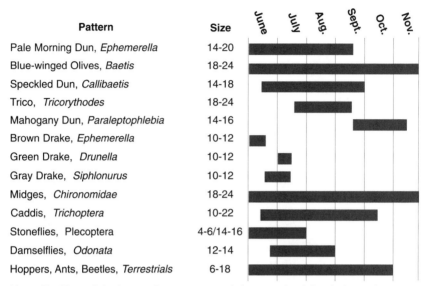

Pattern	Size	June	July	Aug.	Sept.	Oct.	Nov.
Pale Morning Dun, *Ephemerella*	14-20						
Blue-winged Olives, *Baetis*	18-24						
Speckled Dun, *Callibaetis*	14-18						
Trico, *Tricorythodes*	18-24						
Mahogany Dun, *Paraleptophlebia*	14-16						
Brown Drake, *Ephemerella*	10-12						
Green Drake, *Drunella*	10-12						
Gray Drake, *Siphlonurus*	10-12						
Midges, *Chironomidae*	18-24						
Caddis, *Trichoptera*	10-22						
Stoneflies, Plecoptera	4-6/14-16						
Damselflies, *Odonata*	12-14						
Hoppers, Ants, Beetles, *Terrestrials*	6-18						

Notes: Hatching periods often vary by one to two weeks because of variations in the weather. Sizes refer to hook sizes normally used to tie immitation.

panic. To avoid seeing one streaking fish after another while hopper fishing, I generally try to place my first cast well upstream of a rising fish. I let the fly dead drift over the fish. A take at this point is usually as violent as any you will ever see on Silver Creek. Occasionally, however, a take can be just the opposite – raise the head, open the mouth, and let the current carry it in.

The difference between the way rainbow or brown trout take hopper flies, tells you a lot about their personality. Rainbows tend to hit a hopper with everything they have. A brown, on the other hand, is much more reserved. I have often watched browns drift backwards just under a floating hopper fly while inspecting it. Then, if they decide everything looks good, they slowly move to the surface and sip the fly in.

If the fish doesn't strike, I let the fly move past the fish and lightly twitch the fly just before it begins to drag. I have often watched fish turn and shoot downstream to take what it thought was a stick that has now suddenly come to life.

If the first pass doesn't work, I again place the fly as gently as possible on the water at least three feet above the trout. But this time, when the fly is about a foot above the fish, I give it a twitch. If a strike comes, its always explosive.

With the third cast, I am no longer worried about startling the fish and I purposely let the fly slap down about two foot in front of the fish. If the fish doesn't zoom off, the commotion often stimulates the trout into hitting. If the fish holds but doesn't hit, I move on. Hopper fishing isn't like mayfly fishing. After three drifts over a fish, the odds of a strike drop to near zero. When hopper fishing, the a strategy of quickly working the bank and then moving a few yards upstream on every third cast is more effective than trying to thoroughly fishing every square foot of water.

My favorite all around hopper fly is the Joe's Hopper (size 6 to 10). It has an excellent profile, floats extremely well and is a quick tie. Although I haven't seen the variation in any pattern book, tying a one- inch length of elk hair over the back of the body, is a popular tie in southeast Idaho and produces an almost unsinkable fly. In water with a broken surface, such as lower Silver Creek and the Little Wood River, this is the preferred pattern.

For the slow waters of upper Silver Creek, a more realistic pattern is needed. With a nicely shaped head and a very distinctive pair of legs, the Dave's Hopper (size 6 to 12) is a very good pattern. At a distance of a few feet, it is difficult to tell this hopper from a live one. This pattern provides the low-riding, bulky profile and gangly legs of the real thing. The one drawback of this fly is the time it takes to tie. My hat is off to those tiers who can create perfectly spun and cut deer-hair heads required in these flies. Fortunately for me, the trout don't seem to mind the punk-style hairdos of my hoppers.

Beetles

There is no fly like the beetle to match the atmosphere of a hot, July afternoon when the fish are down and feeling especially drowsy. A big, black beetle drifting slowly along, completely motionless is just enough of a mouthful to bring up even the laziest fish.

On Silver Creek, the beetle is the "before and after" fly. Use it in the spring and fall, before and after the hopper. Use it before and after the morning hatch. Use it after nothing else works and before you go crazy.

If you watch the wanderings of a beetle, you get the feeling that the only word in their vocabulary is "whoops!" Whoops! – I just fell off the rock. Whoops! – I just flipped on my back. Whoops! Splat! – I just fell into the water. In the water, these insects are concentrated along the stream edge. Fish them as close to the bank as possible.

I know of one Silver Creek fisherman who one day decided that he was getting nowhere trying to match the hatch. He now exclusively uses nothing but beetle flies. Although I don't know how good a fisherman he was before he changed his tactics, he says he's a better and less frustrated angler now that all his flies are identical.

I have always loved the simplicity and beauty of the Crowe's Beetle (size 12 to 18). Tied with nothing more than a single hunk of black deer hair, it has a perfect body, wing case, head and, if trimmed properly, a set of short legs that look so real, you expect the fly to walk away. The Foam Beetle is another good tie and has somewhat better floating characteristic than the Crowe's Beetle.

Like all black flies, the beetle can be difficult to follow on the water's surface. The recent idea of dabbing a bit of fluorescent or white paint on the shell of the beetle or tying in a small piece of neon-ornage yarn seems to help with this problem and doesn't appear to frighten fish.

Ants

Some experts say trout aggressively take ants because they find the formic acid in their bodies tasty. I guess the tart acid is comparable to garlic, it makes these morsels of food very flavorful. Because trout seem to have a taste for ants and because ants are easy prey once trapped in the surface film, fishing ants can be effectively used all season long.

While ants produce good results when there is no hatch on the water, they can also work well when purposely trying to "mismatch the hatch." When you have one of those days when you just can't come up with a pattern that will entice a fish to strike, try an ant pattern. A narrow-waisted pattern provides trout with an image they have fed on many times before. Because the fish know how easy it is to capture an ant adhering to the water surface, the sight of your imitation sometimes jolts a trout out of its single- minded, pursuit of mayflies.

If a trout passes up a drifting ant, I sometimes wait for it to rise and then plunk the ant right on the fishes' nose. Their reaction is something like a pitcher who snaps his bare hand up to catch a line drive – he wishes he hadn't done it, but by the time the pain reaches his brain, its already too late.

The arrival of a mating swarm of flying ants on Silver Creek is an unusual occurrence and can never be predicted. But since it is one of those rare events that seem to get every fish up and in line for dinner, I always carry at least a few large, winged-ant imitations. These flies may sit in my fly box for several years before being needed, but when flying ants are on the water, good fish are commonly taken.

I have used two ant patterns with good success on Silver Creek. Deer hair ants are easy to tie and provide the bulky, big-butted pattern (size 12) that best imitates the large carpenter ant. Fur ants tied in black, red, and black and red patterns (size 14 to 18) work best in matching most smaller ants.

Amphipoda – Scuds

Scuds are crustaceans (commonly called "fresh water shrimp") that live in the weed masses of Silver Creek. I have watched brown trout forage on scuds by diving into a bed of weeds and then shaking themselves. After breaking scuds loose from the plants, the fish retreat to just downstream where they wait for the plants, silt and most importantly, scuds, to flow past them. From this location, they capture scuds that are being carried by the current.

I sometimes fish a scud pattern as I would a nymph with good results. Fishing with scuds is excellent in the fall as plants die and the scuds are left with less protective cover. On more than one occasion, I have caught a fall trout and watched a steady flow of scuds come out of its mouth while I was removing the hook.

There are several good scud patterns, all of which use clear plastic to form the outside shell and dubbing or hackle on the underneath to indicate a multitude of tiny feet. In olive on a size 16 to 18 hook, with a slight bend at mid-shank, these flies can be very productive in the spring or fall when mayfly nymphal activity is much lower than during the summer months.

Scud

Scuds vary in color , but most fishermen use olive or tan patterns.

Hirudinea – Leeches

Its hard to love a leech. As far as I know, the only animals that look affectionately at leeches are trout and other leeches. But any fly fisherman who has pumped the stomachs of many fish will have at least one favorable thought before being repulsed.

One seldom actually sees a leech in the water. So you just have to assume that they are an important item in the fish diet. For me, confirmation of this fact has come from seeing numerous leeches pumped from the stomachs of trout by biologists who have conducted research on Silver Creek to determine what brown trout eat. I have also found a dozen of them attached to the underside of a wooden fish net (if you can identify it, you can have it back) I rescued from the water near Point of Rocks. Some of these black, flat, wormlike creatures survive by sucking the blood from other organisms, but most eat other insects, mollusks and worms. But as they move through the water with a wavy, undulating motion, they are easy targets for trout.

I have taken more big trout on a black Wooly Bugger than any other fly. When nothing else will work, I pull out one of these mini-Loch Ness monsters and start striping them back. No instructions needed here, the only variations in presentation are how deep you allow the fly to sink and how fast you strip it in. Drifted into bottomless holes and dark nooks and crannies, what these flies sometimes dredge up is amazing.

The traditional all black tie has always worked well for me, but lately I have been adding a few strands of Krystal Flash to the tail for a bit of sparkle. In order to get the fly down, I have switched from wrapping the hook shank with lead to tying this pattern with a bead, or new conehead. I think the heavy bead head gets the fly down and then allows it to imitate the up and down motion of the leech much more realistically as the line is stripped.

Whenever I think I have seen the very last new fly pattern that could possibly be invented, the Orvis catalog arrives and I find I am wrong again. We have seen a multiplicity of fly patterns developed over the last fifteen years as fly tiers have taken a new look at their art and reconsidered color, floatability, silhouette, materials and a dozen other characteristics. We have also seen the number of people who now make a living from testing, developing and selling new flies increase many fold as a proliferation of new anglers flee our cement and asphalt cities and demand the best in trout deceiving illusions. For these reasons, we should expect our choices of usable, creative fly imitations to only increase in the future. Personally, I hope I get the chance to try every one of them on Silver Creek.

The Poly Parachute

One of the most effective mayfly imitations I use on Silver Creek is a fly I refer to as the "Poly Parachute." I take no credit for the invention of this pattern because it is simply a variation of of the parachute style flies Swisher and Richards used as examples in their classic book, *Selective Trout*. Like most good patterns, however, the step-by-step evolution of this fly has gradually lead to a very effective imitation. This simple fly is composed of all artificial materials that owe their existence to the unique characteristics of petroleum; the principle components being polypropylene yarn.

The typical parachute is tied on a standard dry fly hook.

Step 1– First, two microfibetts are tied onto the rear of hook. These nylon bristles, available in a variety of colors, are tied so they point in opposite directions to imitate the spreading tail of the mayfly. A third tail can be added if appropriate. Tip: Tie in one fiber and leave the butt end protruding. Then, when tying in the second fiber, use the butt of the first as a stop to hold it in place while wrapping with tying thread. Then cut off both butt ends.

Step 2 – Then a 1/4th strand of poly yarn is tied in at the rear of the hook and wrapped forward on the shank and secured. Poly dubbing can be substituted for the yarn. Tip: The wrap should extend forward to a point just past the middle of the hook's shank. A substantial space is needed to tie in the wing and hackle without crowding the head.

Step 3 – A short segment – 1/2 strand – of poly yarn is then tied in just in front of the body. This is done by taking a piece of yarn about two inches in length, holding it just under the hook, and then tying it on by making an X of with your thread. Both sides of the yarn are then pulled up above the hook. These are wrapped together with a couple of twists of thread just above the hook to form a post. A couple of turns of thread behind the post will cause it to stand upright like a wing. Tying the wing on in this manner allows you to keep the number of wraps needed to secure the wing to a minimum. Tip: Poly can be easily blended to produce a more realistic, molted wing effect or a mix of colors. Simply hold two strands of poly next to one another and run a bodkin through them until they are mixed into a single strand.

Step 4 – Now a single hackle is tied in and wrapped counter clockwise around the wing post. You should have a good inch of wing material to hold onto while you wrap the hackle. Tip: These hackles should be one or two sizes larger than the gap of the hook. This provides the proper sized "pontoons" to stabilize the fly on the water's surface. It also allows you to use the many of the typical hackles found on less expensive saddle hackle capes now commonly available.

Step 5 – To finish the body of the fly, a small amount of poly yarn or dubbing should be wrapped onto the hook shank just in front of the wing.

Step 6 – After tying off the fly, return to the wing and clip off the appropriate amount. By slanting your scissors down and to the rear when you cut you get a "sail" look to the wing. A second, smaller cut on the top front of the sail, gives a natural profile to the wing. Tip: When making your first cut, leave the wing slightly larger than you feel it should be. Then, relax your grip on the wing and, if needed, make a second cut when the poly is not stretched This techniques will ensure you do not end up with a wing that is too short.

The Poly Parachute is an inexpensive, simple pattern and a dozen flies can be tied in less than an hour The fly is very durable and will outlast many more delicate spring creek patterns that disintegrate on the first fish.

That the fly constantly floats in an upright position can be seen by just tossing one into the air and allowing it to land onto the tying table. The split tail and hackle "pontoons" will cause the fly to land in an upright posture at least ninety percent of the time. The tying material floats extremely well and water logged flies can be quickly dried.

But best of all, the Poly Parachute is capable of deceiving trout. Tied in different sizes and in various color combinations these flies can be made to imitate any mayfly found on Silver Creek. For me, the slim profile and numerous variations, make it one of the few patterns that is nearly impossible to identify as the fake when floating with a bunch of naturals. Silver Creek trout seem to have the same problem.

7
Spring Creek Techniques

Few anglers have experienced anything like a full blown hatch or spinner fall on Silver Creek. The outpouring of blue-winged olives can be so intense that fishermen snort and twitch as they attempt to keep the bugs from walking up their nose or over their eyes. It's during one of these sprees that Silver Creek novices stare bug-eyed as hundreds of fish mechanically bob their heads up and down sipping mayfly after mayfly from the water's surface.

When exposed to such mayfly activity, first-time Silver Creek anglers believe they have waded into fly-fishing heaven. Anticipation doubles the heart rate. Caught between the urge to call friends over to see this spectacle and keeping what they believe to be a once-in-a-lifetime opportunity a secret, the uninitiated angler panics and takes five minutes to tie on a fly. Then – well then nothing. The inexperienced fly fisherman drifts the fly this way and that way. He changes flies like freeway wizards change lanes. In hopes of finding a dull-witted trout, he casts to a dozen different fish. But the strikes don't come.

What is he or she doing wrong? Didn't use the correct technique. What is the correct technique? It's the one that works. How will the angler know what technique will work? When the fish strikes. And when the fish doesn't strike? Try a new technique. And if that doesn't work? Try another.

Sound frustrating? If it does, you have missed the essence of Silver Creek – extremely selective trout that aren't easily fooled are its gift to fisherman. Everyday, sometimes every hour, the game changes – a chess match of sorts where you don't always know the rules and only get brief glimpses of the opposing pieces. On Silver Creek, there are no surefire techniques, there are only some that work better than others.

I offer a few methods that have worked for me. Take what you need, but rely on your own experiences and never be afraid to be creative.

Approach

It's very easy to make your first mistake on Silver Creek before you even get your waders wet. As you push your way through the wild roses, with your attention focused on the wicked thorns, you pop through and damn – a trout bolts away from the bank. Before your first cast, you have announced to every fish in the area, "Here comes one of those big, clumsy, predatory creatures." You have also blown a shot at a bank feeding trout, a fish whose choice of feeding stations makes it a relatively easy target.

You can immediately improve your chance of success by using a quiet, stealthy approach when fishing Silver Creek. Begin using this strategy as soon as you near the edge of the stream. Walk cautiously and take your first look at the stream while still several yards from the bank. Don't let the urge to cast a fly rush you into the water.

From a discreet distance, try to determine where the fish are located. The concentric circles of a rise are a good clue, but many fish don't leave such tell-tale evidence. Often the big fish are the most dainty of feeders and disturb the surface less than a 1-inch minnow when taking an insect.

Look for the top of a head, a dorsal fin, or the last inch of a tail cutting in rippled water where riseforms break quickly. Look for a fish nabbing insects within a couple of inches of the streamside cattails where surface waves quickly disappear as they reach the vegetation. Look for the nose of a fish that is holding just an inch or two under water and shows only the tip of its snoot when rising to seine insects from the surface or sub-surface. Look for the fish that aren't rising – shadowy shapes on the stream's bottom.

Try to determine what the insects are doing. Can you identify anything floating on the surface? Is there a swarm of mayfly spinners flying overhead? Are caddis bobbing in the air near the sides of the stream? Are any of the terrestrial insects grasshoppers, ants, beetles – active? Are damselflies performing their incredibly clumsy mating routine that leaves them floating in a heap on the surface?

Finally, when you have determined where the fish are and, if possible, what they are feeding on, decide what your ideal fishing position would be. Note the location of the sun and be sure to locate yourself so as not to "spook" fish with

Calm, reflective water offers special challenges.

your movement or shadow. Consider the surface glare reflecting off of the water and how it will affect your ability to track a floating fly. Check the strength and direction of the wind, and place yourself so the breezes work for, not against, you. Determine the current pattern; try to avoid taking up a casting position where you have to work across more than one tongue of current. Taking the time to think all of this out on every new section of stream you enter takes a lot of discipline, but with experience it becomes a ritual that lasts only a minute or so.

Now you're ready to drop your boots off the edge of the undercut bank, right? Wrong! Although you will need to get into the water to reach most fish, remember that wading always creates waves and kicks up silt and vegetation that drift downstream, putting feeding fish down. Always try to fish to any trout within casting distance from the bank first. Only when opportunities for fishing from the bank are exhausted, is it time to get wet.

Getting In and Moving About

How you enter the stream can greatly affect your fishing success. How would you feel if you were in your favorite easy chair when an earthquake hit? Would it affect your behavior if your house trembled and the roof collapsed around you? This may be what a trout experiences when a fisherman jumps into the water, thrashes around, pulls up bootloads of mossy vegetation, and finishes by stirring up a thick, muddy, milk shake of sediment.

If the water is too deep to gently step into the stream, then sit down on the bank, swing your legs over the water and softly step down. If you don't see the wakes of a half dozen fish radiating away like the spokes of a wheel, you are probably doing it correctly. In the water, move slowly and, if possible, walk over gravel instead of silt. On Silver Creek, the channels between weed beds are often deep enough to funnel most of the murky water and debris downstream in a narrow path. If you walk in one channel and fish in the adjacent channel, you can often keep from deluging your target in a shower of debris. Often, to reach the best position for fishing to a particular fish, you may need to buck thick weeds as you push fifty feet upstream, work through a long bed of sucking muck, stomp through a maze of cattails and muskrat holes, climb out over a mud-slick bank, and push through a tangle of willows. After finding those obstacles, you may only find yourself entering the stream only a few feet from where you started. But if this is the only route that leaves the fish undisturbed, it's the only choice you have – gut buster or not.

Silver Creek fish may give the false appearance of being accustomed to the constant presence of fisherman. While it is true that you can sometimes wade through a group of feeding fish and turn around in a couple of minutes to find them rising again, you will usually find that every fish is just beyond casting distance. Move a few yards towards them, and, unless you move with the stealth of a blue heron stalking its prey, the rise-forms will disappear again just as you get within range. One of the first lessons you need to learn is that, while Silver Creek trout seldom panic when they realize you are nearby, they will often quit feeding or at least become much more difficult to fool.

Fishing Downstream

Most anglers are trained at birth to cast upstream, so it may seem odd to start by talking about fishing downstream. Fishing downstream, however, is the most commonly used technique on Silver Creek. This is due to the inherent difficulty most fishermen have in fishing a stream having numerous currents that travel at different speeds and in vari-

Serpentine cast. Wiggle rod end.

ous directions. These various currents are created by plants, small islands, and a bottom that's six-inches deep in one place and six-feet deep in another. Within the larger currents, there are also numerous micro- currents that can be very difficult to see. These multiple currents can wreak havoc when trying to cast across the stream. Fishing downstream is usually the most effective way to restrict your drift to a single current and thus eliminate drag.

Another advantage of fishing downstream is that your fly will reach the trout's position before your tippet so the trout always sees the fly first. Also, if you cast at a slight angle to the downstream flow, its easy to maneuver your tackle so that the leader and line are kept away from the trout's position and only the fly and the tippet float directly over the fish.

When directing a leader downstream, it's also easy to work

your fly around and through numerous patches of vegetation that peek through the surface and create leader-entangling obstructions. Fishing in these obstacle courses is much easier when you put your fly into the large, upper end of a current and then allow it to direct your fly into the narrow slot of fast water between the weeds.

Another situation where downstream fishing is a better solution is when the wind is blowing downstream. This often occurs at Silver Creek because the stream travels from predominantly west to east and the prevailing wind most often comes from the southwest. Thus the wind blows downstream most of the time. Given a choice, you should try not to buck the wind. It's always better to move to a position where the wind will work for you.

When casting downstream, any slack line cast will work. In a light wind, I keep the rod tip high and bring the line to an abrupt stop in the traditional method for creating a slack-line presentation. If the wind is forcing the line to carry too far, I execute the same cast, but drop the rod butt abruptly toward the water. This forces the line down faster and with more authority, but still creates a slack line. If the wind is extremely strong or I want very long drift, I will sometimes use a wiggle or stutter cast. By wiggling the rod tip back and forth, side to side, large S-curves can be put into the line as it falls to the water.

Skate Cast

A cast made just for Silver Creek is the skate cast (I have also seen this called the slide cast). Using the skate cast an angler can drift a fly with complete precision. It is not unusual to become so adept at this presentation that you can consistently float a fly through a space no wider than the distance between a trout's eyes. The skate cast is accomplished by casting the fly downstream across the current so that it lands approximately three feet or more beyond and above a rising fish. You allow the current to pull the line taunt and then slowly lifting the rod tip, the line and most of the leader is then picked off the stream's surface. At this point, lifting the rod too fast can drown the fly, but if the line is raised slowly and steadi-

Skate cast

ly the dry fly will skate across the surface of the water. When aligned properly with the current or a feeding trout, the rod tip is dropped and the fly and leader allowed to float downstream. Dragfree drifts of ten feet or more are possible if slack line is held loosely in the hand and then fed forward through the rod guides with short flicks of the rod.

Using this technique, the fly can be placed into the exact center of the tiniest current and delivered right into a trout's feeding lane. Control can be so exact that you can literally slip a fly into an awaiting trout's mouth.

When fishing downstream and your fish won't strike, it's important to allow the fly to drift well beyond the trout's position before you start your retrieve. Dragging your fly upstream across the back of a fish is a sure way to send it on its way to, eventually, the Pacific Ocean. This cast is also an excellent one for correcting any cast that has gone a bit too far. The errant fly can be pulled back into the feeding lane on a taunt line and then released to float drag free to the awaiting trout. The cast can also be effectively used to fish to a line of fish, where after a refusal by one, the fly is drug into the proper position to entice the next fish in the dinner line.

Because positioning a skating fly causes a bit of commotion and can easily drown flies, this method is usually only used when a traditional downstream cast will not work. This usually happens when deep water or an obstruction keeps you from getting close enough to the fish to put it into that magic six-inch circle. Under these circumstances, it is just sometimes easier to pull a fly into position than it is to get an airborne one to hit the spot.

Skating and Twitching

The technique for skating/twitching a fly is exactly the same as described for the skate cast. This time, however, you are not trying to locate the fly in just the right spot, but rather trying to duplicate the behavior of a mayfly or caddis.

When fishing a mayfly or caddis hatch, a skittering or skating fly can often out perform a dead drift presentation. Twitching the fly in conjunction with a dead drift may also trigger a reaction. This movement imitates the action of a mayfly dun fighting and fluttering in an attempt to get off of the water. It also imitates the behavior of a caddis fly dashing across the water's surface towards the bank.

Rapidfire Casting

Rapidfire casting is what I call the quick, repetitive movement where, as soon as a fly has passed over a trout's position, the line is backcast into the air and then immediately thrown forward for another drift. This method is characterized by a total lack of false casting.

This style of casting is used during prolific hatches and spinner falls when a steady stream of insects is floating on the creek and the fish are in a full head- bobbing, feeding-frenzy mode. In this situation, a fish rises rhythmically while taking an insect every few seconds. The quick motion of the single cast allows you to consistently get your fly into a position immediately in front of a fish nearly every time it surfaces. If your fly is a good imitation of the real thing, the fish are just as apt to take it as any of the naturals. The Trico spinner falls lend themselves best to this type of machine gun action.

And so the game begins – everything has to be perfect.

Watch the fish. Time the rises. Get the rhythm. Set the fly down three to four feet in front of the gaping, white mouth. Allow the fly to float for at least three yards. If the trout doesn't take the fly make one quick backcast and immediately cast to the same location. If you stay with it long enough and the fish continues to rise, everything will eventually come together.

When a fish finally gulps your fly, there is a real sense of having done something that required perfect timing and precision – and when was the last time you did anything that was perfect?

Fishing Upstream

Although taking a backseat to the downstream presentations on Silver Creek, under the right conditions, upstream fishing can also be very effective. A major advantage to an upstream approach is that it provides the best hooking angle. From behind the fish, the act of lifting the rod will drawn the fly hook back into the crook of the trout's mouth. Since trout do not

see well to the rear, another plus in fishing up current is being able to move in closer to your target without fear of spooking it. This allows you to make shorter and more accurate casts and helps you keep small flies in sight.

Occasionally the traditional upstream cast that quarters across the stream, will allow for the fly presentation you are seeking. Traditional casting methods such as the stop or curve cast work well at times, but the secret to executing a good upstream cast on Silver Creek is in positioning

Fishing upstream to a bank feeder.

yourself so that your line will cross as few currents as possible and in reducing the chance of lining the fish with the use of a longer leader and tippet.

When fishing upstream, the best casting position is often directly downstream from the fish. Your goal when using this technique is to drop your fly and only a couple of feet of your tippet directly in front of the trout without scaring it. Casting upstream and directly over the fish allows you to keep your fly, leader and line within the same current and improves your chance of achieving a drag-free float. Accomplish this without spooking the fish and you have truly earned your Silver Creek wings.

You can also improve your chances of keeping the trout from sensing what you have done by timing your cast to land just after the fish has risen. If the fly and tippet lands within the dissipating rings of the rise, the fish seldom recognizes the slight disturbance. Drop your fly on flat water and the fish may be gone.

To be successful, your cast must be right on the button. If you cast too far, you risk dropping the heavy section of your leader or even your line right on the trout's head. If you cast short, it's the fly that may bonk your quarry on the noggin. For the perfect delivery, start by casting short dropping your fly on the water just behind the trout's tail. When you can hit this target, reach down and feed out three feet of line. Now your line is exactly the right length to put you fly two feet upstream of the trout.

This type of upstream cast should also be considered when fishing for bank feeders. While you can often make a perfect drift from upstream, if the trout doesn't take on the first cast, your retrieve will bring your line directly over the fish. On the other hand, by casting over the fish from the downstream side, your line stays away from the fish and, if the fish doesn't strike, the fly just flows away on the current. You can cast time after time from this position.

Fishing Across Stream

The reach cast usually works best when you have no other choice but to cast across more than one current. My jaw went slack when I first saw this simple cast so effectively solve the drag problem that results from casting across more than one current. This cast was taught to me by Richard Parks, a Yellowstone guide out of Gardiner, Montana.

This cast is accomplished by making a standard throw that ends with your pushing or reaching the rod across your body. For reasons only known to fly fishing physicists, the belly of the line always curves upstream, preventing the instant drag so common when using other casts. In effect you are

Reach cast

throwing an "aerial mend" in mid-air. This is also a good cast to use to pitch a fly to a bank feeder when you can't get to a down-stream position or when trying to get a few seconds of dragfree drift in that calm water that is sometimes found on just the other side of strong current.

In cross-stream fishing the practice of mending (flipping the mid-section or belly of the line upstream to prevent drag) can also be an important tool in making a good presentation. I find that I usually mend once just as the line touches the water and then as needed as the line floats downstream. When mending, I often see anglers make the mistake of flipping the line upstream without letting any additional line out. When this is done, it is worse than not mending at all because you will be tightening up the line more instead of less. Always hold a small loop of line in your non-casting hand and release this every time you mend the line.

Nymphing

While Silver Creek's reputation is built on its incredible top water fishing, you will have many fishless days if you always depend on dry flies. You will also miss out on a lot of enjoyable fishing.

Because Silver Creek is not the classic type of nymphing water – there tends to be fly-grabbing vegetation nearly everywhere – many anglers ignore the possibilities of sub-surface fishing. But before, during, and after a hatch, fishing nymphs can produce phenomenal results.

When fishing the lower section of Silver Creek a lack of heavy vegetation allows you to use traditional nymphing techniques. Primarily, this means you can cast your fly upstream, allow it to drift downstream while lifting your rod tip, and then, when the fly has drifted past, you can drop your rod tip until the fly reaches the end of its drift and rises to the surface. Under these conditions, you can also weight the fly or the leader to get your nymph to sink. More interesting to most Silver Creek fisherman are techniques that work in the weed-packed waters where you usually must fish in the top foot or two of water and can seldom attach a weight.

There are several techniques that can be used to fish the upper level of water. By casting five or six feet upstream of a feeding trout and locating the nymph as it lands, you can follow the position of the fly by watching the leader as it drifts with the current. If a dead drift doesn't produce a hit, a gentle twitch or pull on the line just as it approaches the fish will often result in a strike. If this doesn't work, try stopping the line just short of the fish and giving it a series of short jerks. This will cause the nymph to move upwards as if it were struggling to reach the surface. If this action triggers a trout to strike, you will always feel a jolt.

Usually, you can watch the very end of the tippet where it enters the water for that small movement that tells you to lift the rod and set the hook on a trout. In some cases, treating a short section of tippet four of five inches above the fly with floatant keeps the leader riding higher on the surface and makes it more visible. If lighting conditions still make it

difficult for you to see the leader, however, a piece of yarn or
strike indicator can be tied on to your leader to make it easier
to follow.

I hate to admit it, but although I use the yarn much of the
time, I also use adhesive, stick-on strike indicators as well. Not
as esthetic as the yarn – they remind me of mini-beachballs –
you can attach or detach these very quickly. I don't think the
fish are spooked by their less than natural appearance. One of
the nymphing techniques that has had impressive results on
Silver Creek involves attaching a strike indicator to the tippet
just six to twelve inches above the fly. Normally, you would
assume that placing a strike indicator so close to the fly would
scare fish away, or at least the nymph would act so strangely
that a trout would have nothing to do with it. Well, you know
what they say about making assumptions.

I first started using this technique when frustrated by fish
feeding on nymphs just under the surface which is very, very
common on Silver Creek. In this situation, emergers were
ignored and, when I cast them a few feet ahead of the fish, they
would sink to a depth below – even though unweighted, the
nymphs would drop below the trout's feeding zone before it
reached them—where the feeding activity was taking place. If I
tried to keep the nymph up near the surface by setting the
nymph down only a foot or so in front of the rising fish, the fish
would frequently scatter. The lack of strikes also made me wonder if my fly was dragging or acting non-insect like underwater.

One day, after hours of watching bulging fish totally ignore
my every presentation, I attached a strike indicator just above
a small pheasant tail nymph and landed the outfit about three
feet upstream from the fish. I didn't get a strike on my first
pass, but I did on the second. It seems this setup allowed me to
put the fly into the water well above the trout while the strike
indicator kept the fly from sinking more than an inch or two
under the surface.

With only a few inches of tippet beyond the indicator, a take
is never difficult to identify. Just like in bluegill fishing, the tiny
yarn bobber suddenly pops below the surface. You just lift and
there's your fish.

I've noticed that fish that don't strike will usually continue to feed, even when the indicator passes directly over them, indicating fish are not generally frightened by the strike indicator. I have also noted that this technique is often a trip saver when the water is so calm that fish seem to find a problem with every dry fly you throw.

I'm not sure, but I think is possible that using the strike indicator may also result in a more natural looking drift of the fly. When using this technique, I can see any drag by looking at the strike indicator. A quick mend and the fly is back to drifting naturally again.

Although I first used the strike indicator technique only when fishing to trout feeding just under the surface, I have since tried it with fish I know are also taking duns or spinners on the surface. So far the results have been encouraging. Apparently that old axiom that trout feed on nymphs ninety percent of the time applies to Silver Creek as well. I guess classic flyfishing tradition makes me feel a bit guilty about using this technique. And I do feel guilty – right up until I see the strike indicator go under. Then I feel the same excitement I experienced as a six-year old boy watching my red and white bobber being pulled under water by silver dollar- sized, yellow perch. The magic of a strike is so powerful that little else seems to matter – no matter how old you are.

Another nymphing technique that works well is just a skate cast with a nymph. This technique involves locating a feeding fish and then casting a nymph to a position beyond and upstream of its position. Once the nymph has entered the water, the rod tip is lifted and the line and leader are tightened and straightened. When you do this, the fly immediately begins to drag or skate across the water's surface. By maneuvering the fly toward you, it is possible to move it to a position directly upstream of the trout. Again, this cast is made downstream and quartering across the current so that the leader and line are kept as far from the fish as possible.

To avoid spooking the fish, the dragging fly should be kept at least three feet above the trout. Once the nymph is lined up, you slowly lower the tip of your rod and drift the fly to the awaiting fish. This can be done in several different ways that all produce slightly different results. One way is to drop your rod tip quickly while feeding out slack line which allows the nymph to sink a foot or more by the time it reaches the trout on a dead drift. Another is to drop your rod tip and move it downstream at the same speed of the drifting fly without feeding any line out which keeps a slight amount of tension on the line while the fly is presented to the fish just a few inches below the surface. A third way is to quickly feed the fly to the fish in a dead drift presentation and then raise the rod tip when the fly is approximately one foot in front of the trout's position. This method combines the previous two techniques into one; the nymph rises toward the surface directly in front of the trout and then, when the rod tip is lowered again the fly drifts just under the surface to the feeding fish.

When using this third presentation, if a fish hits while the line is tight, you typically feel only a quick jerk as your fly pops right out the trout's mouth or you might feel a tremendous jolt capable of separating you from your fish and fly. If you keep yourself prepared for the strike, you can sometimes apply just that perfect amount of pressure that will hook the fish while preventing a break off.

Sight nymphing is another very effective technique at Silver Creek. By wearing polarized sunglasses and moving slowly upstream – so the fish don't see you and dart away along the bank, you can often spot trout feeding just below the water's surface. Walking on the bank gives you the advantage of being able to look from above into the stream, but care needs to be taken to keep as far back from the stream as possible and use the grass, willows, and shrubs for cover.

Lighting plays a big role in spotting and stalking trout lying on the stream bottom. Depending on the angle of the sun, one side of the stream may offer you a much better view of submerged trout than the other. To locate your quarry, look for those places where the sunlight isn't radiating off the surface, the water is shallow, and the bottom is covered with light-colored gravel. These conditions create windows that allow you to see into the depths and spot the dark silhouette of a fish.

Once you have located a trout, move to a position where you can cast to it and, if possible, keep it in sight. As your nymph approaches the fish, watch for any movement; the white flash of an open mouth or the quick flare as a fish suddenly moves forward or rotates onto its side. If you see either of these indications, lift the rod to see if it was your fly the trout dined on. Using a gentle lift insures that, if the fish didn't go for your nymph, you won't spook it and can get a second chance.

You will find that most fish taken with nymphs strike close to the surface, so sinking the fly deep is seldom necessary. If you

Beadhead

must get the fly down, attaching weight to the leader is preferable. Nymphs tied with lead wrapped around the hook drift like an anchor. Depending on how much weight is needed, split shot or micro shot can be used to get your line down. The weight is usually attached to the tippet approximately eighteen inches from the fly. This distance should be adjusted to whatever position gets the fly down to the proper depth and still allows for a somewhat natural drift.

Presentation can be greatly improved if you try a test cast away from your target and watch how the fly behaves as it drifts by you. A sense of how quickly the fly will sink and move with the current, with or without weight, will give you an advantage when trying to place your nymph into a knot hole-sized mouth at ten feet.

The recent and almost phenomenal resurgence of the bead-head has many fishermen using a fly that is rapidly replacing many of the nymph patterns that are now weighted by winding a length of lead around the shank of the hook. Developed in Europe in the late 1930s, the fly has again gained popularity all over the United States. Just as the Royal Coachman is an attractor dry fly, the bead-head is an attractor nymph.

The beadhead is tied by pushing the point of a hook through a small hole in a brass or silver bead. The bead forms a collar just behind the eye. A body that mimics a Hare's Ear, a Pheasant Tail or any other nymph pattern is tied on the shank of the hook behind the bead.

The bead provides the weight needed to get a fly down quickly and its placement on the front of the hook gives the fly a distinctive pulsating motion as it is stripped back. The bead makes this fly a well-balanced projectile that is easier to cast than a traditionally weighted fly and much easier to cast than an awkward fly-tippet-split shot rig. A final plus, is that the metallic bead provides just a flash of reflected light that may be an important stimulus in getting a fish to strike.

As the beadhead hits the water, you have the choice of immediately stripping it back or waiting for it to sink to various depths. Strikes seem to come more regularly when the fly is stripped back with three to four- inch tugs.

Tracking and Concentration

Having chosen the proper fly, presented it with finesse and ultimately fooled a trout into striking, it's a shame to miss the fish because your attention is somewhere else. If you lose track of your drifting fly or if you loose your concentration, the odds of hooking a fish are almost nil. I have to admit to hooking fish while wading with my line and fly dragging in the water, having fish hit while I restrung my rod in midstream, and once, when trying to climb onto the bank, having the rod set the hook after I had laid it on the bank with the water tugging at the fly and line. But until I perfect these techniques, I can't recommend them.

You need to know what your fly is doing at all times. Locate your fly as soon as it hits the water. This is easy to do if you're fishing a Royal Coachman Trude, but with the minuscule flies used much of the time on Silver Creek, it is often difficult to see your imitation. The easiest way to make a fly easy to spot on a sunny day is to tie in some white material; polyprophelene, CDC feathers or calftail are good choices. On overcast days, everything changes and black colors may be much easier to see.

If matching the hatch won't allow for the use of a bright or dark-hued pattern that could be easily seen, there are other ways to improve your ability to see a fly. Get into a position where the reflection of sunlight off the water works for you. If the glare off the water makes it impossible to see your floating fly, move to where the reflection or shadow of the nearby hills or bankside willows create a dark spot on the water.

When the sun is low and you are having a difficult time seeing your dark fly on the black surface of the water, do just the opposite – find that spot where the sunlight makes the water sparkle. When a fly floats through these areas, it can often be seen in profile as it throws a small shadow from being backlit. Another technique to track your fly is to cast your fly so it lands very close to something – a leaf, fluffy cattail seed, bubble or an authentic bug – that is easier to see and follow. And if there is absolutely nothing floating on the surface, immediately point your rod tip toward where you think the fly landed. Then move your rod tip at the same speed you estimate the fly to be drifting. This last technique can also be used when drifting emergers or nymphs under the surface.

One other method of keeping track of your fly involves the use of a strike indicator. Although normally used for nymphing, this method can also be used when it is impossible to see your fly on the water. When using a low riding, dark fly (eg. Trico spinner) that can be difficult to see, you can add a strike indicator to the butt of your leader and use it to determine when a fish takes.

Concentration is necessary to insure you strike at just the right instant. There are only two kinds of concentration: partial and total. With partial concentration, you notice the mallards flying over, watch mayflies crawl up you waders, and spy on other fishermen to see if they are catching fish. You also miss more strikes than you hit, will be loved by the fish, and collect enough trivial information about aquatic ecosystems to become a good outdoor writer. On the other hand, if you have total concentration your sunburnt face and migraine headache testifies that you are indeed a fishoholic. You never notice that your waders are leaking until the end of the day and, unless you can find someone to talk to about fly fishing, you find cocktail parties unbearably boring. You're loved by slow-moving insects because you hook lots of fish and keep them occupied for long periods of time, hated by your fishless companions, and don't have to make up nearly as many fish stories when you get home. I find the happiest fishermen are those that alternate between both mental phases; they smell the roses, but occasionally pluck them as well.

Hooking

Considering the small hooks used for the match-the-hatch type of fishing Silver Creek requires, it's no wonder that many fish are just pricked or missed outright. Capturing a large fish with a size 24 hook is something like shoveling an Idaho snowfall with a teaspoon; it can be done, but it's not easy.

When fishing downstream, your line is usually more taunt than when fishing upstream. Because of this, when you get a hard strike on a light tippet, the result will most often be an immediate break off. In order to prevent as many of these breakoffs as possible, remember that the light leaders used on Silver Creek demand that you never strike, you lift. If you're accustomed to fishing big flies on heavy leaders it takes awhile to get the touch. Just remember, don't jerk, elevate!

The speed with which you strike is especially important when fishing downstream. If you set the hook too quickly, there is a tendency to pull the fly out of the trout's mouth without ever contacting flesh. Hesitating slightly, until the trout has sunk below the surface, allows the fly to move a bit further toward the digestive system and increases the chances of a good set. Wait too long, however, and the fish will spit the fake fly out like a wad of chewing tobacco.

Upstream presentations provide the best hooking angle because when the fly is pulled back into the trout's mouth it often wedges in the corner of the jaws. Even when fishing upstream, it is still generally better to hesitate until the trout's head is again beneath the surface before lifting the rod to set the hook.

I've certainly missed my fair share of fish by setting the hook too quickly. One miss that still haunts my memory occurred while fishing hoppers on a hot August day. I had moved through a tall stand of willows to the edge of the stream and found myself standing just above of a deep, undercut bank. With no room for a backcast, I decided to make a bow and arrow type presentation by pulling the Dave's Hopper, arching my rod, and then letting the fly slip out of my fingers. After release, the fly flew about ten feet and plopped onto the water.

Suddenly, I saw a dark shadow move out from beneath the bank. It was literally at my feet. I watched the fish creep towards my fly. The fish was so close I could see its dark eyes and every spot of what must have been a seven-pound brown trout. Cautiously, the brown stuck its nose within one inch of my hopper. But it didn't strike.

Slowly, very slowly, the brown trout allowed itself to drift downstream with the current at the exact speed as the floating hopper. After three or four seconds, or at least enough time for me to visualize myself landing this fish several times, the trout was in a position immediately in front of me. I couldn't mend my line, take in slack line or even breath.

With only a few inches of drag free float left, the brown moved slightly forward and scooped up my fly. By this time, I was frazzled and my heart was pounding. It's one thing to take a fish at twenty feet and quite another to take one at twenty inches. My brain said take your time, while my instincts screamed pull! My instincts won and I lifted my rod so fast the rod slapped the willows behind me and the fly smacked me in the face. The behemoth didn't panic, it just slipped back into the dark bowl beneath the bank. It's been many years since this encounter and every time I relive the experience, I wait one more second before setting the hook. If football is a game of inches, then fly fishing is a game of millimeters.

To improve the odds, there are a few things you can try. Use the expensive, chemically-sharpened hooks or make sure to touch up your points with a sharpening stone. Your hooks should be so sharp they can be used to split atoms.

Another strategy that will sometimes increase your number of hookups is the use of large-gap, short-shanked hooks. Looking a lot like the salmon egg hooks I used as a kid, a fly tied on these hooks has a standard sized gap but a shank that is shorter than normal. In other words, a size 16 hook will have a shank length equal to that of a size 18 hook. It used to be that you had to purchase hooks made for tying "spider flies," but now some companies specifically make these type of hooks.

Another trick is to use a hook that is larger than the insect you are trying to match, but tie two flies on it, one on the rear of the hook and a second on the front. This is an especially effective Trico imitation, where the trout love to get two for one when spinners carpet the water.

Playing

When I set the hook and touch a big fish, one of four things usually happens. A few fish do absolutely nothing. Possibly, they have never been hooked before or, just the opposite, they have been hooked so many times, another sharp jab in their jaw doesn't seem to be cause for panic. Either way, I have hooked many fish that initially respond with what could best be described as a tremendously fierce sulk. With these fish, if I had not applied pressure and forced the issue, I don't think they would have ever gotten excited. When you do put tension on the line, however, these fish are likely to stay deep and shake their heads from side to side. Its like playing tug-of-war with a dog.

Another group of fish respond with an immediate leap. I can recall encountering such a fish during a very light hatch of pale morning duns at one of my favorite pockets of water near The Nature Conservancy visitor center. I was drifting parachute imitations to any of a half dozen sporadic sippers. None of the fish seemed too excited and, since none of the trout appeared to be in the foot or better class, my own response was rather lethargic.

Finally, a fish half-heartedly rose and took my fly. Since the dimple left by the trout's nose was smaller than a silver dollar, I didn't expect much as I elevated the rod, but the vision of what happened next still wakes me up in the middle of the night.

Instantly, upon feeling the hook, the rainbow launched itself in the air. The jump wasn't the high, vertical leap of a small fish or the trashing, splashing swirl of the larger fish. It was an honest-to-God, horizontal broad jump of at least twelve feet. From a standing start, this fish catapulted itself forward in an arc that peaked only eighteen inches over the water.

The fish was airborne for so long, there was plenty of time for a string of thoughts – He's 30-inches – There's my fly in the corner of his mouth – I've got on 7X – When he hits the water, that'll be it.

Actually it didn't even take that long for the fish to break off. The rainbow's leap was so far and so powerful, the leader was immediately jerked out of the water. When the entire length of leader cleared the water, the trout's momentum pulled it tight and tugged at the line. The heavier line, which couldn't move at the same speed as the fish, was dragged through the water and the resistance became too much for the light tippet. The fish popped my line while still airborne. The entire experience lasted only a second or two, but I no longer determine how large fish are by the size of the divot their nose makes when they sip a fly off the surface.

The third response is tail-wagging. The fish dunks its head just under the surface while its skyward-pointing tail waves from side to side. The fish never moves from where it is hooked, but the tail movement is so violent, a bowl two feet in diameter forms as water is sprayed in every direction. Tail-wagging never lasts for more than a few seconds and is usually followed by a streaking run.

The last response is a distance burning run. I know of no sound as pleasant as the zit-zit-zit of a fish burning line off of your reel. Enough said.

When you pull back on a good fish, you never know which of these responses you are going to get. It doesn't matter though, since the proper counter move is always the same – do as little as possible. After you set the hook, except for those ill-tempered, bottom hugging brutes, you will nearly always experience a five to twenty second, all-out surge as the fish struggles to free itself. Whether the trout's reaction is one solid, knot-breaking jerk after another, or a 100-yard dash designed to out-run the problem, any attempt by you to contain the fish will be a disaster. This doesn't mean that you shouldn't apply pressure to the line to slow the trout's run, but rather that the risk of a break off is much larger if you try to turn, or stop, a trout dead in its tracks, or better, dead in its wake.

During the initial run, only two responses have a prayer of working. The first is to let the fish pull line out as fast as it can. Slow the line for a micro-second by catching a loop over a finger, snagging the line on your leader nippers, or letting it get wound around one strand of weeds and you can immediately start looking for another fly. The second tactic involves holding your rod up as high as you can reach. This reduces the drag on the line and keeps most of the line off the water and out of the weeds. This technique also puts tension onto any limp line and allows you to begin to reel in excess line.

As soon as the fish slows, you need to get any slack line onto your reel. The best way to play a fish is off of the reel. A reel with a good drag is the only way you can steadily feed line out with consistent pressure. It's just impossible to match this precision by pinching the line between two fat fingers. If the trout decides to run in your direction and creates a lot of slack line, raise your rod tip high into the air and quickly strip the line – don't try to wind it onto the reel. As soon as the fish changes direction, reel the line back in.

There are days on Silver Creek when you may do everything right and still lose every hooked fish to the weeds. Fortunately, there are a few trout that never realize the advantage of plunging into the line-fouling mass of vegetation. You can also encourage every fish to fight on the surface by applying steady pressure and keeping your line high and taunt. The more pressure exerted with the rod during the fight, the less chance the trout will have to burrow into the vegetation. Holding the rod at a high angle will also keep the trout closer to the surface and provide better control.

If a fish and your leader become caught in the strands of vegetation, ease up. Once a fish gets into the weeds, you can't just yank it out. You need to get downstream and try to guide the fish out the backdoor. If that doesn't work, with only your leader and a foot or so of line beyond your rod tip , try to ease the fish back toward you. Since you're pulling in the direction of least resistance, there is a chance the fish can be backed out of its green tunnel.

If this tactic doesn't work, move in closer and follow your line into the vegetation. If you spot the trout, don't try to pull it out by tugging on the line. Reach down just in front of the fish and try to scoop it into a weedfree area with your hand. While trying to sweep it out of its refuge you may lose the fish, but at this point you don't have a lot of choices.

If you find the trout is too deep to reach, the tactic of last resort is to get above the fish and walk toward where you think it is hidden. Occasionally, you can spook the fish out into open water.

And even if you lose a trout to the weeds, so what. Some of the best Silver Creek fishermen I know are only average anglers, but they have elevated the ability to lose fish to a new art form!

Landing Fish

Besides inflating your ego, the objective of landing a fish is to allow the trout to return to the stream to fight another day, so always do whatever is best for the fish. Landing small fish is easy. Quickly pull the fish to the surface, grasp the fly with a set of forceps or one of the new hook removers, and, with a quick twist, flip the hook out. If the fish doesn't need to be resuscitated, you will never touch it or remove it from the water.

As you get ready to land a larger fish, anticipate a final, panicky dash when the trout spots you or your net. When bringing the fish in close, avoid bringing the leader into the guides. If the trout decides to run at the last moment – which they always do the connecting knot between leader and line is destined to snag on a guide and cause your tippet to snap. When you sense the fish is finished thrashing around, take in enough leader to allow you to reach the trout. If the fish turns on another burst of energy, immediately drop the rod tip and ease off and reduce the tension.

A larger fish that will need to be revived should be landed by using a net. The best technique for netting your fish is to manoeuvre it upstream, dip your net underwater just behind the fish, then slowly let the fish drift with the current until it is directly over the net. A swift sweep and the fish is subdued. This technique is effective because the fish doesn't see the net until it is too late and, if you bump the fish and it tries to escape, the current will help push it back into the net.

Catch-and-Release

Catch-and-release regulations apply to all of Silver Creek within The Nature Conservancy property and most fly fishermen release fish taken anywhere on the stream. There is a problem though, in that many anglers think that as long as they release their fish, they are off the hook (pardon the pun)—and have done their part to preserve quality fishing. Well, when four to nine percent (or more depending which study you read) of all released fish die soon afterwards, it's obvious that we all need to do better job.

Here are a few tips to increase the chance the fish you release will survive:

• Use the Strongest Possible Leader
    Landing a big fish on light leader can be a test of your skill, but enlarging your ego is never an excuse for killing a fish. While there are days when trout will back away from any fly that is tied to anything but an extremely fine tippet, the use of these hairlike strands should only be done with the understanding that all fish will be landed quickly.
    Fighting a fish until it is belly up allows large quantities of lactic acid to build in the trout's tissue. If this toxin reaches a relatively high level, the fish can be temporarily revived, but will die shortly after release. To avoid this, a trout hooked on a lightweight tippet must be aggressively played. If the tippet breaks, this loss is accepted as the price paid for insuring the trout will be around for another battle.

• Bend Down Your Barbs
    This seems like an obvious and unnecessary request. In fact, since barbless hooks are a requirement in all catch-and-release waters, why should I insult you by bringing it up? Unfortunately, some people are just not complying with the law. Fish and Game officers who float through the stream in canoes, report that they cite more people for having barbs on their hooks than any other infraction.
    To prevent forgetting to bend down barbs, do it at your fly tying bench. If you bend the barb down before beginning to tie and the hook breaks under the pres-

sure of a pair of pliers, you haven't wasted your time tying up a worthless fly. You may occasionally lose a fish because a barbless hook pulls out, but this momentary disappointment is far outweighed by the satisfaction of releasing your fish unharmed. A hook that can't be easily disengaged endangers the life of every fish you catch with it.

• Carry Forceps

Forceps or a hook remover should be used for extracting flies from the mouth of a fish. With these, a small fish doesn't even have to be taken out of the water. Just reach down and remove the fly. On larger fish, these tools still work better than your fingers because you don't have the fear of embedding a hook in your hand.

• Carry Clippers

Carry a set of clippers that can be used to clip a tippet when a fish is hooked too deeply or in a critical area. And use it – a fly that cost less than two dollars is not worth salvaging at the expense of a trout's life.

If a fish is deeply hooked in the throat or gills, cut the line immediately. If a small fish is hooked in the upper maxillary, cut the fly off rather than take the chance of damaging the trout's jaw. For a trout, losing this fleshy bone is a little like having your own upper lip ripped off – it may not kill you, but it's not going to make your day.

• Use a Net

If you can easily remove a hook from a trout's jaw while it is in the water, do so. Trying this with good sized fish, however, usually results in an embarrassing wrestling match and only prolongs the time the fish is tethered to your line. With a net, you can contain fish so that they are handled less and don't get their internal organs damaged by squeezing.

• Hold Fish Properly

If you have to lift a trout, don't squeeze down. When lifting, put one hand under the trout's belly at the junction of the head and body. The other hand supports the fish just ahead of the tail. Never, never allow your fingers to touch the gills. I have always found that turning a fish upside down seems to have a calming effect and makes it easier to handle panicky trout.

• Revive Fish Properly

If you must take a fish out of the water, be sure to return it to the stream as soon as possible. Think about how much fun it would be if the tables were turned; if a fish

Holding fish for release.

hooked you while you walked along the bank, dragged you under the water and then held your head underwater for a couple of minutes – not a pretty picture is it?

If a fish does need to be revived, hold its head into a strong current until you feel the trout's energy return. When the trout can swim off under its own power, release it. After the fish has moved off, continue to watch it until you're sure it isn't going to go belly up or get stuck in a weed bed. If this occurs, collect the fish in your net again and resuscitate it again.

• Enlighten Others

Most Silver Creek anglers do the "right" and legal thing by releasing their fish, but don't really know how to do this so that the fish ends up with all its parts still working. If you see an angler hold a fish out of the water for several minutes to film or photograph their catch, stick their pudgy fingers into the trout's gills, apply a death grip around the trout's belly, or return the fish to the water with an unthinking toss, put on your most pleasant smile and inquire, "I have a slightly different way to handle and release fish. Mind if I tell you about it?"

In summation, after talking so much about different approaches that work on Silver Creek, I will let you in on a secret; every technique works some of the time and no technique works all of the time. The fun is in the search.

8
Fishing Holes

The "classic" view of Silver Creek

I have yet to see a magazine article about Silver Creek, including my own, that did not include a photo of the meandering stream taken from the hill behind The Nature Conservancy's log cabin visitor center. This pastoral scene is symbolic of Silver Creek (it was recently used on a poster) announcing the benefit dinner and auction – an annual event held in Sun Valley, Idaho, to raise funds for the Silver Creek Preserve.

A framed copy of this portrait of Silver Creek now hangs on my office wall. I seldom look closely at the poster until well into the depths of the long, Idaho winter. Then, when it's cold enough to freeze a sneeze in mid-air, I look longingly at this image that has captured the very essence of Silver Creek.

Every year, new discoveries demonstrate to me that to assume that all of Silver Creek resembles this quiescent setting is to judge a person's character by their physical appearance. Although most fishermen are mesmerized by the placid, slow-moving water of Silver Creek within the boundaries of The Nature Conservancy, those that explore the entire stream find holes so deep you need several split shot to get a streamer to the bottom, pockets of fast water where you can bounce stonefly nymphs between piles of boulders, and swamplike backwaters where, when the wind is calm, a dry fly is anchored wherever it lands.

Headwaters

Stalker Creek

Stalker Creek should appeal to you if you're an expert caster, a good fish stalker, and a bit of a lunatic.

First the bad news. This narrow, headwater stream is a place where fishing involves a lot of sweat and frustration. When fishing here, you must carry your rod butt end first as you creep through tangled willows. This is a place where, as you force your way through the bushes, it's not the showy, aromatic flowers of the wild rose that catch your attention, but rather its needle-sharp thorns.

As soon as you step off of the bank into Stalker Creek (the Conservancy only allows fishing in the section of Stalker Creek downstream from the Stalker Bridge), you realize this is going to be tough fishing. First, you can never stop moving when wading here. Leaving your foot sunk into the deep silt and decaying vegetation for more than a few seconds allows the muddy mixture to ooze up your leg and firmly anchor you to the bottom. You can only remain mobile by making sure to pull your boot out of the mud every few seconds. Unfortunately, every time you lift your foot, a storm of debris and chocolate mud are stirred up and cloud the water for thirty yards downstream.

Another problem on Stalker Creek is that you typically find yourself fishing in a tunnel of green vegetation. If you find losing a few flies to appease the bush gods annoying – this is no place for you. Here, you keep your casts short and precise or head back to where the stream is wide, the bushes farther apart, and where everyone else fishes.

On the other hand, if you're one of those anglers with the ability to cast with mathematical precision and a desire for something a bit different, fishing Stalker Creek can be a real pleasure. To be successful, all you have to do is realize that this is one-fish-at-a-time water. You look for a feeding fish and then cast to it until you take it or spook it. If you can't catch the fish in front of you, you aren't going to take the one around the bend. This is specialized fishing where patience and persistence are at least as important as any other skill.

Another plus concerns the recent arrival of the brown trout in Stalker Creek. The deep, undercut banks and abundant over-hanging vegetation found here create a gloomy, sunless envi-ronment loved by the browns. You can often take good brown trout during the day by drifting big flies deep into the deep holes. In the late evening, browns can be taken in more open water as they move out from under their cover to feed.

If you take a fish on Stalker Creek – even if it is only an eight-incher – your reward is a sense of satisfaction that there aren't many other fly fishermen who could do the same.

Grove Creek

Rising from the ground west of Pumpkin Center Road near the town of Gannett, Grove Creek travels south through private property, crosses Highway 20, and continues through more pri-vate property to meet Stalker Creek within the Conservancy. Where these two creeks join, Silver Creek is born. Grove Creek is the primary spawning tributary for Silver Creek trout. With very little silt and a gravel bottom, this is perfect habitat for spawning rainbows and browns.

From March through early May, rainbows run up this spring creek in great numbers and can be seen all the way up to the bridge at Pumpkin Center Road. Most of these trout drop back into Silver Creek after spawning with only a few residing in the deeper pools or runs for the summer. This is a beautiful little creek and fishing can be good on those years when fish numbers are high. It is very important to respect the rights of private landowners along this stream.

Loving Creek

No living creature has the ability to destroy the natural world like man and, not to be a chauvinist, woman. And even though it occurred way back in 1907, when the Hayspur Hatchery was being built, the funneling of Loving Creek into a series of raceways and a newly constructed canal, is proof that regardless of the era, bad judgement is always a possibility. Concerned only with raising fish, the determination to destroy what must have been a beautiful stretch of stream was carried out by the very people who should have recognized its value.

Fortunately, when they want to, people also have the ability to reverse the impacts of their bad decisions. In a six year effort, the Idaho Department of Fish and Game and several local fly fishing organizations excavated 9,100 cubic yards of gravel and stone and diverted the water of Loving Creek back into its original channel. Regulations that allow for only two fish over twenty inches in length to be taken have been enacted on this section of stream in order to establish this creek as trophy trout water.

This portion of Loving Creek is within casting distance of the Hayspur Hatchery and campground. Seldom wider than fifteen feet, the stream looks much too small to support anything that would approach a trophy trout. But looks are deceiving.

The fishable portion of the stream starts just below the hatchery's main holding pond (sometimes containing as many as 3,000 fish). The stream is over four feet deep in places, has beautifully sculpted banks and plenty of vegetation that provides cover to some very large residents. Reports of anglers taking twenty-inch fish here are common.

The largest fish I have seen in this water spent a bright sunny August day slowly rolling onto the surface in a slack water area about the size of a bathtub. Time-after-time, the rainbow I estimated to be in the five-pound category pushed its way through a quarter inch of lime-green algae as it sucked down something it found interesting on the surface. Not having a fly that worked well in slime, I couldn't seem to get the fish interested in my offering, but I certainly developed a whole different opinion about the potential of this 500-yard long piece of water.

Besides the occasional big fish, Loving Creek holds plenty of respectable trout in the twelve- to eighteen- inch class. During the season, these fish can be found actively feeding on mayfly and midge hatches.

Loving Creek is a wonderfully tough place to fish. If you get into the stream to position yourself for a downstream drift, you find that the solid looking gravel bars have no bottom. Step on to the coarse quicksand and you slowly sink until the water is an inch or two above the top of your waders. In the places where you can wade, the mud you kick up will quickly put down every downstream fish.

Reduced to fishing up or across stream while crouching or kneeling on the bank, you have to be able to drop a fly into a coffee cup at twenty feet. No problem you say. Well, then try doing it into a fifteen mph wind.

This miniature creek epitomizes fly fishing difficulty and challenge. Take a couple of fish here and you demonstrate that you are an expert fly-fisher.

Mid-Loving Creek

As Loving Creek leaves Idaho Fish and Game property below the Hayspur Hatchery, it flows south through private property, crosses Highway 20, and runs across more private property to join Silver Creek within the Silver Creek Preserve. Trout populations in this area tend to be high and fishing here can be good. There is a pond area downstream of Highway 20 that is created by a small dam and irrigation canal headgate. This pond often holds large rainbows which move upstream as water temperatures rise during July and August. In this area, it is critical to respect private property and stay within the high water marks.

Lower Loving Creek

Lower Loving Creek is delineated by a bridge and fence at its upper end. There is about 500 yards of fishable water between this point and where Loving Creek enters Silver Creek. The stream bottom here is extremely silty so the best results are usually obtained when casting from the bank.

Loving Creek is best when fished early in the season because by August, it is choked by plants that stretch from bank-to-bank. In early summer, however, this is some of the best midging water anywhere in the Silver Creek drainage. If fish are rising, but you don't see any insects on the water, it's safe to assume they're feeding on midges. This can usually be confirmed by checking to see if midges are swarming at the edge of the stream.

At first look, midge-feeding fish appear to be breaking through the water's surface and a dry fly or emerger pattern seems to be the obvious choice. But catch a trout, pump its stomach, and the results often say something else. By a ratio of about ten to one, Loving Creek trout seem to prefer midge pupa. Because every rise breaks through the surface, however, it's a sure bet that the fish are taking the pupa in the surface film just before emergence.

When fishing an imitation of a midge pupa, concentrate on the rise pattern of an individual fish and then cast your fly to land about twelve inches in front of where the trout last rose. By keeping the drift short, the fly will have sunk only an inch or two beneath the surface by the time it reaches the trout.

You can try this technique with or without a strike indicator on your line. As your fly drifts through the dissipating rings of the rise, you just assume that any movement of fish, tippet, or strike indicator means the fish has inhaled your fly. Much of the time you will be wrong, but occasionally – bingo!

Spring Fed Lakes

Sullivan Lake

Sullivan Lake, created by the collective flow of several different springs, is located just a few hundred yards west of The Nature Conservancy's visitor center. Originally created by beavers, the water level of this pond has now been stabilized by reinforcing the dam with sand bags.

If the wind is calm and the water's surface isn't distorted, you can often watch large, cigar-shaped fish silhouettes cruise over the light-colored bottom from the hill above Sullivan Lake. If you don't see rising fish, you're in for some tough nymph fishing. If the trout are rising, you're in for some tough dry fly fishing. In fact, "tough fishing" is probably the best way to describe what most anglers experience on Sullivan Lake.

The primary hatch in Sullivan Lake is the Callibaetis. Once this hatch starts in late June, it occurs with great regularity in the late morning for nearly the entire summer. Since Callibaetis tend to spend relatively long periods of time floating on the surface (they have a rather stupefied approach to life) trout seldom get too excited about chasing these tidbits. Trout usually take the Callibaetis in slow motion with porpoising rises or with a string of head bobbing maneuvers done as the fish picks off a succession of one mayflies after the other.

Extreme patience is an absolute virtue when fishing Sullivan's because the best way to fish this hatch often involves doing absolutely nothing. First, you pick a spot were several fish are sporadically rising and cast your fly into their midst. Then you wait. Or you throw your fly up against the edge of an island of vegetation where the Callibaetis spinners are being pushed by the slightest puff of wind. Then you wait.

You know you'll be a good Callibaetis fisherman if you can keep right on smiling when you just miss catching the green light at an intersection. You have the potential to be a great Callibaetis fisherman if, having had to wait through three rotations of the stop light to even get to the intersection, you miss the green light again and still have a sense of humor. Since I live in a town without a single stop light, it's difficult to measure my tolerance for frustration, but I do know that I don't have enough composure to let my fly sit absolutely still for more than one minute. Whether leaving my fly completely stationary for longer periods would produce more strikes, I'll never know – after sixty seconds of watching fish take everything but my fly, I always crack and recast.

The best fishing on Sullivan Lake occurs when a hatch is

accompanied by a good breeze that causes the surface of the water to be rippled or even choppy. Under these conditions, microscopic tippets are no longer needed and your choice of potential fly patterns is greatly expanded. When the wind is blowing, fly floatability and the ability to see your fly become the most important factors. A parachute Adams tied with some white in the wings and a few extra wraps of hackle often work very well under these conditions.

A broken surface makes it easier to fool a rainbow into a take, but also increases the difficulty of spotting rising trout. Distortion of the surface also means it will be nearly impossible to see a fish beneath the surface. This is where experience and knowledge of the routes these trout patrol pays off.

If your target fish isn't following a predictable route, you should always cast your fly to the upwind side of the spot where the fish last rose. By doing this, you place your fly so that the wind will push it through and beyond the rise. This presentation provides you with an opportunity for a strike on either side of the trout's last position.

The lightest of breezes cause natural mayflies to drift across the water's surface, thus your fly must also respond properly to the air currents. If your fly is anchored to a plant by your leader, trout won't ambush your dead-in-the-water offering. When fishing where weed patches are close to the surface, you should dress your leader and tippet with a floatant. This keeps your leader on the surface and doesn't allow it to sink into the vegetation and impede the drift of your fly.

During the non-hatch periods on this lake, nymph fishing is about your only option for taking these fish. With the aid of polarized sun glasses, the best technique is to sight fish for trout that are actively searching for nymphs. Just like fish looking for insects on the surface, nymphing fish also follow a habitual beat. By observing the trout's movements you will eventually be able to predict what route they will follow.

Once you have determined the trout's cruising pattern, you want to wait to toss a nymph in front of a fish as it makes its rounds. When the fish comes to within a few feet of the nymph, you twitch it toward the surface with short jerks and then allow it to sink. If no strike occurs, the nymph is slowly retrieved with four-inch strips in hopes that the fish will aggressively attack.

The slow-motion fishing on Sullivan Lake during Callibaetis hatches provides plenty of time to reflect on past fishing experiences. I frequently have flashbacks about a huge rainbow trout that would pop its entire head out the water by rising straight up, nose pointed toward the sky. On its way up, the trout would open its mouth, take a mayfly, and then slowly allow itself to slide beneath the surface again.

The fish scoffed my every offer, but because the rainbow was a good four inches from his eye to the tip of his nose, no number of refusals would deter me from trying again. Finally, I guess a neutron in the trout's brain missed its mark or I was being rewarded for changing that old woman's tire during a snow storm, but, whatever the reason, the head burst through the surface to inhale my Callibaetis spinner imitation.

The fish immediately made a thirty-yard dash and launched itself into the air. The two-foot fish cleared the water by twice its length. When it came back to earth – no, water – my 6X leader snapped. That particular vision makes it impossible for me to ever pass up trying Sullivan's when the fish are rising.

One word of caution before fishing Sullivan Lake. Much of Sullivan's bottom is silt and getting too far from the shore is not a good idea. I know one fisherman who tried to wade from one side of Sullivan Lake to the other. Let's just say that when he looks for excitement today, he knits himself a sweater or cuts the lawn. A word to the wise – there are only a few places where you can wade across Sullivan Lake and a lot of places where you can't.

Lower Slough

A spring fed pool called the Lower Slough flows into Silver Creek just above the pond above Kilpatrick Bridge. As you make the short hike from the road to Silver Creek along a well established trail, you will probably ignore the Slough on your first few visits, but eventually curiosity will get the better of you. One day, you will take the detour through the reeds or the brush to get to the pond. Most of the time, you won't see much happening, but occasionally, you'll be greeted by dozens of the expanding circles produced by hungry fish.

If the rises are perfect concentric rings and you can see a few large, dark mayflies floating on the surface or light colored mayflies dancing near the shoreline, the trout are probably feeding on Callibaetis duns or spinners respectively. Just as on Sullivan's Lake, the fish here pick off one mayfly and then move on to search for the next one. On the other hand, if you see a small swarm of little black flies bobbing up and down near the shoreline and notice that the fish are forming two- to three-foot wakes as they swim along just under the water's surface, it is likely they are seining midges. Splashy, violent upheavals indicate that a rainbow has invited a damsel fly to lunch.

While the occurrence of Callibaetis hatches on the Lower Slough is similar to those on Sullivan Lake, midge hatches are much more extensive here. The Lower Slough is perfect midge habitat because the bottom consists of mud and more mud. Technically, I guess this is silt, but on the bottom of my boots, this black, gooey stuff is "mud," which seems to be an appropriate description.

Midges are generally too small to be seen as they ride on the surface, but they can be identified fluttering around near the shore or in the gill rakers or mouth of a captured trout. For a fly pattern, any small (18 to 24), dark-colored "thing" usually does a good job of imitating the real "thing." The only decision to make is usually whether to imitate the emerging pupa or the adult insect.

Fishing to these fish is totally different than fishing to creek fish. These fish don't feed in one location and wait for the current to carry their food to them. These fish are cruisers, and while they know where they are going, the trick is for you to determine what their next position will be.

As the fish moves into range, it will pop up in one place, disappear, then surface again, five feet away. If you can keep track of an individual fish for long enough, you can usually figure out whether it is right or left handed (or is that finned) and so favors turning clockwise or counterclockwise after feeding. Often it's just guess work.

This can be frustrating fishing. Here's the typical scenario.

Fish rises. Cast fly to left. Fish rises right. Cast right. Fish rises left. Cast long. Fish rises short. Odds say you will pick correctly one in four times. Reality says fat chance. If having a plan is important to you, forget fishing the Lower Slough.

The Slough seems to have been designed to frustrate the angler. The Slough's floor is too mucky to allow wading more than a few feet from shore and, since The Nature Conservancy has outlawed the use of float tubes here and has made the north shore area off limits to protect the wetlands, it is difficult to reach much of the Lower Slough's water with even an extra long cast. This wouldn't be a problem if ninety-five percent of the trout didn't spend ninety-five percent of their time rising just beyond casting distance – ninety-five feet away!

On the Lower Slough you will have to contend with tall, fly-snagging bushes and the tall, tippet-fouling tops of the tall stalks of Giant Wild Rye found in this area. You are left with two choices. You can become adept at throwing long casts from the bank or you can seek out areas where the wind has blown the naturals into the bank. The trout follow these insects into shore and they can often be found taking insects within a few inches of the edge. A careful stalk to the border of the pond and a short, precise cast can often bring better results than trying longer casts to trout in the middle of the pond.

When there are no Callibaetis or midges in the vicinity, the use of an adult damsel fly may be a good choice. I particularly remember the sight one July day of a rainbow prowling just a few feet from my casting position on the bank. I had just tied on a size 12 fly that imitated the cobalt-blue, male damsels that were flying near the edge of the Slough. As I dropped my fly onto the water, it landed much closer to the fish than I had intended. Actually, I bombed the big, blue damsel right down on top of the trout's head.

But the fish didn't spook. Instead, moving in slow, slow-motion, the trout eased toward the surface. I swear I could see the tiny wheels moving in the nineteen-inch rainbow's head. The trout's tail was dead still as it gradually floated upward. I expected the fish to turn at the last moment because I didn't think the large, hunky damsel fly could hold up to this close inspection. But apparently the trout was satisfied that it was looking at a genuine mouthful of delicious damsel.

The fish continued to rise towards the surface with all the speed of roadkilled rabbit. Suddenly, a quick flick of its tail and the trout shot forward and engulfed the fly.

With no more than fifteen feet of leader and line out, the trout made one of those swishing, back-and-forth tail waves when hooked by my forceful lift. When this didn't result in freedom, the fish made a run of forty feet, jumped once, and then dove deep into the weeds. The next thing I knew, I had on a soggy damsel fly, six inches of green slime, and a one-of-a-kind memory of a beautiful take.

Portions of the Slough can be fished all season long, but near the end of summer, the heavy growth of vegetation makes much of this water impossible to fish. As it spreads, the aquatic bloom eventually squeezes many of the trout out of the Slough and back into the main stream. In late summer, fishing the Slough is a bit like trying to fish on your front lawn.

Silver Creek

The Nature Conservancy

The upper section of Silver Creek is that area that lies within the boundaries of the privately owned, Nature Conservancy's Silver Creek Preserve. In this classic spring creek water, the major difficulty for most first-time fishermen is to determine where fish will hold in this nearly unvarying flow of water. With experience, you soon realize that, depending on what the insects are doing, trout prefer very specific types of lies.

Just as on fast-water streams, trout seek out those places where there is an abundance of food, protective cover nearby, and places where the water slows. Good water includes anywhere structure – reeds, bushes, banks – projects into the stream and creates a good hold for trout on the downstream side. Islands provide ideal places for floating insects to accumulate in the pockets of still water on the downstream side. On the stream's outside curve, the current often carves a foot-wide path between the weed beds and bank that provides a perfect lie for opportunistic feeders. The jagged edge of cattail patches serve as a windbreak that provides a backwater where the current slows and where spent spinners accumulate after a hatch.

But the most important lies are within the channels that run through weed patches. These chutes funnel huge amounts of food to waiting trout and the thick forest of vegetation allows a startled fish to quickly disappear like a kid burrowing into a pile of autumn leaves. This combination provides some of the best holds in the entire stream.

With a reputation for incredible hatches, this section of stream attracts more fisherman than any other place on the stream. Huge hatches are so thick that mayflies can actually be a distraction as they climb around your eyes, wander up your nose, or are inhaled into your mouth – the relative size of a hatch of blue-winged olives can be measured by how many times you have to spit one out. Most fishermen who observe a full blown, multiple hatch of mayflies on Silver Creek say they have never seen anything quite like it.

The list of mayflies found here includes several species of blue-winged olives, pale morning duns, Callibaetis, Tricos, and mahogany duns (I don't know why Silver Creek anglers refer to some of these mayflies by their Latin monikers while calling others by their common name). Some of these insects hatch out at site after site along the entire length of the stream while others are more selective and prefer more specific habitats.

While fishing wadable water with mayfly imitations keeps the majority of anglers who fish The Conservancy happy, there are some who approach this area a little differently. For example, there are anglers who only fish deep water. On Silver Creek, deep water is any place deeper than the top of your waders and is typified by the section of stream that everyone calls the S-Curves. The S-curves are a short section of water about one-fourth-mile long immediately upstream of the pond above Kilpatrick Bridge. Access to this area is pretty much restricted to float tube users because of the deep water and the fact that The Nature Conservancy has closed a major section of the bank to use in order to prevent further trampling of the vegetation.

The most unique thing about fishing deep-water areas is the size and composition of the fish found here. Here, undercut

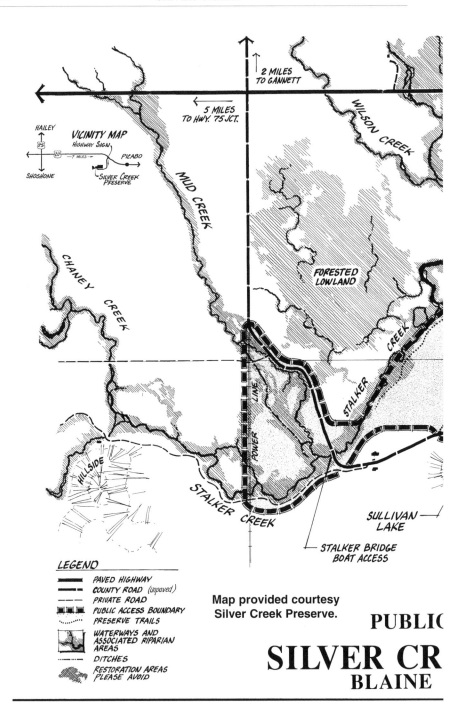

2 MILES
TO GANNETT

5 MILES
TO HWY. 75 JCT.

WILSON CREEK

VICINITY MAP
HIGHWAY SIGN
HAILEY
75
20
7 MILES
PICABO
SILVER CREEK
PRESERVE
SHOSHONE

MUD CREEK

CHANEY CREEK

FORESTED
LOWLAND

STALKER CREEK

POWER LINE

HILLSIDE

STALKER CREEK

SULLIVAN
LAKE

STALKER BRIDGE
BOAT ACCESS

LEGEND

PAVED HIGHWAY
COUNTY ROAD (unpaved)
PRIVATE ROAD
PUBLIC ACCESS BOUNDARY
PRESERVE TRAILS
WATERWAYS AND
ASSOCIATED RIPARIAN
AREAS
DITCHES
RESTORATION AREAS
PLEASE AVOID

Map provided courtesy
Silver Creek Preserve.

PUBLIC

SILVER CR

BLAINE

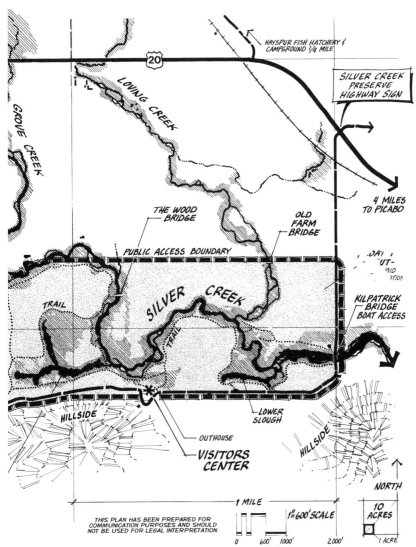

HAYSPUR FISH HATCHERY &
CAMPGROUND 1/4 MILE

20

SILVER CREEK
PRESERVE
HIGHWAY SIGN

4 MILES
TO PICABO

GROVE CREEK

LOVING CREEK

THE WOOD
BRIDGE

OLD
FARM
BRIDGE

PUBLIC ACCESS BOUNDARY

KILPATRICK
BRIDGE
BOAT ACCESS

TRAIL

SILVER CREEK

TRAIL

HILLSIDE

HILLSIDE

LOWER
SLOUGH

OUTHOUSE

VISITORS
CENTER

NORTH

1 MILE

10
ACRES

THIS PLAN HAS BEEN PREPARED FOR
COMMUNICATION PURPOSES AND SHOULD
NOT BE USED FOR LEGAL INTERPRETATION.

1"=600' SCALE

0   600' 1000'   2,000'

1 ACRE

ACCESS MAP

EEK PRESERVE

COUNTY, IDAHO

The
Nature
Conservancy
OF IDAHO

banks and dark channels provide the ideal lairs for huge rainbow and brown trout. Rainbows are still the predominant fish
in these deep waters. However, the brown trout head toward the
top of their population curve in this habitat where they hug the
stream bottom while remaining hidden from predators. I would
estimate that four times as many browns are caught in these
deep waters than anywhere else in the Silver Creek Preserve.

To take brown trout in Silver Creek, it is important to
understand how the behavior of this fish changes as the season
progresses. During the spring and early summer months, the
browns tend to hold in deep holes and undercuts during the day
and then move into shallow water at night when protected by
the cover of darkness. As a result, most of the browns caught
during June, July and August are hooked as dusk approaches or
even after dark.

In early fall, browns seem to become a little more aggressive during the day. This may be a reaction to the return of
lower water temperatures, the coming of the spawning season,
or an attempt to beef up on insects before the long winter
arrives. The offering of an autumn grasshopper is often greeted
by the appearance of an impressively self-assertive brown trout.

Later in the fall, browns prepare to spawn by moving into
the upper stretches of Silver Creek where they build their redds
on the scattered beds of gravel.

How big is a big, Silver Creek trout? The largest rainbow I
have landed in The Nature Conservancy was a twenty-five-inch
red-sided male taken on a damsel fly imitation within spitting
distance of The Nature Conservancy visitor center.

The largest brown I have taken in the Conservancy was a
twenty-seven-inch female of about seven pounds taken in the S-
curves. I spotted this fish while walking along the bank. I
dropped a beadhead hare's ear to the bottom and led it right up
to the trout's mouth. Ten, twenty, thirty drifts. Then, when I
finally saw the fish move forward, I lifted the rod and was fast
into a huge hen brown. The fish headed deep like most browns,
but after fighting for a couple of minutes, suddenly launched
itself into the air. An airborne, heavy fish is quite a sight and a
little out of character for brown trout. The fight gradually
moved fifty yards downstream where I was finally able to

maneuver the fish into one of the few shallow areas in this area. It was here that I saw that my hook was imbedded one inch from the back edge of the trout's tail. The hook looked like it was about to pull out at any time, and, since I had forgotten to bring my net with me, I asked my companion to help me land the fish. He put on a wool mitt so he could get a good grip on the fishes tail and played gillie.

For some reason, a foul-hooked fish is always somewhat less of a trophy than one caught in the lip or mouth. I know this particular fish was initially hooked in the mouth because I saw the tippet hanging from her head during the spectacular jump. It's still a mystery to me how my hare's ear finished up at the trout's other end. Regardless of where the brown was hooked, it was a great fight and a fantastic fish.

The giant of Silver Creek so far seems to be the thirty-inch brown I heard was taken in 1995, again in the S-curves. This fish was caught by a friend who I consider to be very truthful. Besides, he had a witness.

Up to now, I don't know of anyone who has taken a fish of better than thirty inches anywhere on Silver Creek. But I do know fish of this size or larger exist here. I have talked to biologists who have electro- shocked fish and have brought up browns as large as twelve pounds or have snorkeled through Silver Creek and come face to face with equally large fish. The largest trout I have seen was a brown I estimate at better than thirty inches. I watched this fish chase an eight-inch rainbow round and round in a shallow pool. With the brown's dorsal fin sticking out of the water as it rushed one way and then the other, it looked like a small shark had been set loose in Silver Creek.

It is true that I am no longer on a mission to catch Silver Creek's biggest fish. But if by some accident the behemoth should somehow choose my fly to strike, please Lord, let me have just cut back my tippet to 4X.

The Pond

Below Kilpatrick Bridge, on private property, is a small wooden-plank dam built to funnel irrigation water into Kilpatrick Canal. This dam creates the lakelike impoundment

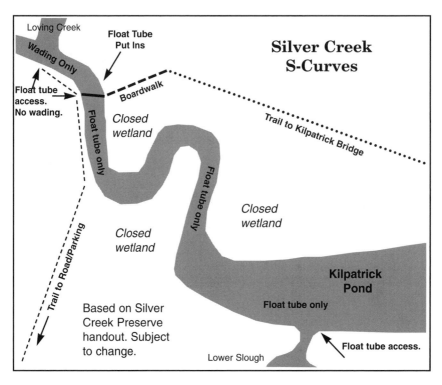

on both sides of Kilpatrick Bridge referred to by anglers as the "Pond."

As silt laden water enters this large pool just below the S-curves, the current slows and the suspended debris sinks forming an ultra-mucky streambed. Nearly bottomless in places, the mud makes it dangerous to try a crossing in this area. Fortunately, float tubing is allowed in this area or there would be no access to this superb water.

Plenty of different mayflies hatch on The Pond, but the slow-water loving Callibaetis is one of the predominant hatches. During any given Callibaetis hatch, trout can be seen doing any of a half-dozen different things. Some wait patiently in good lies and take spinners or duns with a splashy rise. Some cruise large areas actively searching for targets. Some work subsurface nymphs. Some linger at the edge of the reeds and simply rock backwards, tilt their head up, and allow Callibaetis to flow directly into their gullet. Some head into pockets of water surrounded by cattails to pick up spent spinners and some gather in small, bathtub-sized openings in the middle of the weedbeds where they patiently pluck off the occasional speckled wing. Like a van full of kids arguing about which fast food restaurant to stop at, every fish seems to have its own opinion on how to best enjoy the Callibaetis feast.

Of all the hatches on Silver Creek, the emergence of Callibaetis may be the one most loved by fly-fishers. This predictable, long-lasting hatch of large mayflies is capable of getting every fish in the stream up and feeding, giving the fly fisherman hours of enjoyment. Being able to relish this hatch while sitting in a overstuffed chair of a float tube makes fly fishing an absolutely heavenly sport within a sport.

The Double "RR" Ranch

Downstream of Kilpatrick Bridge, Silver Creek flows through the famed Purdy family ranch known as the "Double RR" or Picabo Livestock Ranch. Through a conservation easement with The Nature Conservancy, much of this section of the stream has been fenced to keep grazing cattle out of the creek. This greatly helps stream bank restoration and the reduction of siltation problems.

This stretch of Silver Creek is completely on private property and the only access is from the Kilpatrick Bridge and Highway 20. Float tubing is common in this area and is an all day affair due to the distance involved If you put in at the bridge, with the exception of encountering an obstacle that can not be safely floated over or around, you cannot leave the stream until you exit at the highway (see sidebar on public access). To drift through the ranch means floating over two miles of stream.

A few lucky anglers have drive-in access to this ranch and you need to be careful not to float over water others are fishing. It's always best to give way and ask which way to float around other wading or float tubing fishermen. Plan for a minimum of six hours to make this trip and, if the hatches are good, at least eight hours.

Hatches in this section of Silver Creek are much the same as upstream in The Nature Conservancy.

Point of Rocks

Silver Creek East, is more commonly known as "Point of Rocks." This location was named for a prominent rock monolith located between Silver Creek and the base of the foothills of the Pioneer Mountains. This section of Silver Creek can be reached by taking the road just south of the Gannett turnoff on Highway 20 or by taking the road just west of the Picabo General Store. Both of these roads are marked on the highway by "Sportsman Access" signs.

It is easiest to reach the upper section of stream by turning off Highway 20 on a gravel road that arrives within 500 yards at a four-way junction. By turning to the right and heading through a tunnel of willows, you quickly come to a dead end that is distinguished by a single water pipe spanning the stream. This pipe marks the site of a bridge (when it existed, it was known as Martin Bridge) that, until just a few years ago, allowed access to the other side of the stream. I remember the very day this bridge gave up the ghost – it was the tire of my truck that fell through a plank in the bridge and signaled that maybe, even by Idaho standards, the bridge was a bit old.

Fortunately, instead of repairing the bridge, the Idaho Department of Fish and Game decided to remove it. This decision to limit vehicle access saw the well-trampled habitat rapidly improve as the roads, paths, and campsites that once scarred the banks of Silver Creek disappeared within only a few years. Its almost magical how the land so quickly returned to a natural condition (excluding a few exotic plants) when people are not allowed to take their 3,000-pound mechanical friends everywhere.

At the dead end, you have the option of getting out and fishing directly downstream or taking a second road that exits just before you reach the dead end. This road follows along the north side of Silver Creek along land owned by the Idaho Department of Fish and Game for about one-half-mile. The stream here is deep and moves slowly through a near cave of shrubs and trees.

Except when the water levels are at a maximum, most of this section of Silver Creek can be waded. Having a good set of tippy-toes sometimes helps in some of the get-wet holes. An alternate strategy to wading is to fish from a float tube.

However, anglers should always be leery of getting pulled by the current into overhanging willows and losing control of their tube.

This place reeks of big browns. Here there are plenty of dark abysses, stretches were branches hang a good four feet over the water and lots of dark, undercut banks. Several anglers have proudly shown me photos of five-, six-, and seven-pound brown trout taken in this water in late evening or even after dark. Taken with a flash, all you see in the photo is a black background, a huge fish that takes two hands to hold, and the beaming smile of a person who thinks fishing at night is something normal people do.

Regardless of how good the night fishing can be, I have found just as many large browns can be taken with the right timing and technique during the daylight hours. Early in the season, size-6 Wooly Buggers slipped deep under the hollowed out banks will produce the occasional strike. In mid-summer, large, hopper flies drifted within a few inches of shore may occasionally lure browns out of their lairs. In the fall, when browns begin to crowd into the area to spawn, colorful streamers will often irritate hook- jawed males and round-bellied females into hitting.

Unlike many of the hook-and-bullet writers, I won't make it sound like taking these big fish happens on a regular basis. When using these methods and fishing strictly for big browns, I feel one or two strikes represents a good day. The taking of a single good fish may take many hours of fishing over a period of days, weeks, or even months – yes months! After all, persistence, accompanied by the rationale, "If I wasn't spending my time doing this, I'd probably be in jail, divorced, or in detox" keep me coming back so that even I occasionally take one of these really big fish.

The character of Silver Creek changes as soon as it exits the tunnel of vegetation. Downstream, the creek widens and flows between banks alternatively covered with grass and low-growing shrubs or marshy areas. Great hopper fishing exists wherever meadow-like conditions are found.

Immature hoppers that appear in late-June are best imitated by small, size 12 flies. By July these insects have grown dramatically and size 8 and 10 imitations are used. August brings on the big hoppers. Now imitations are tied on 8, 6 and even 4 hooks.

With all of the hype about the fantastic Trico hatches on the upper creek, it's amazing how little you hear about the black-and-whites on this water. But as on the Silver Creek Preserve, this section of the stream can see Trico hatches so extensive nearly every fish will be up and feeding. Heavy Trico spinner falls can even pique the interest of otherwise shy brown trout. For the fisherman who takes the time to look for the slurpers rather than the sippers, several twenty-inch plus browns can usually be located over the course of a spinner fall.

I can't end these comments on the Point of Rocks area without a few words about the brown drake hatch. Depending on how quickly the weather warms up in the spring, this hatch occurs sometime from late-May to mid-June. These giant mayflies are only found here during an emergence than usually spans a period of two weeks. During this time, the peak of the hatch will occur on only three or four days..

Unfortunately, this hatch nearly always starts very late in the evening – usually after 8 P.M. Although this hatch takes place during some of the longest days of the year, the sun still sets by 9:30 P.M. and, by the time the mayflies emerge, there isn't much daylight left for fishing. At the height of the hatch, fishermen may drive for many miles only to have the mayflies come off long after the sun has gone down.

During the uprising of brown drakes, the best fishing usually occurs near the beginning of the hatch. Even when only a few of these mayflies are on the water, the trout are quick to respond to these one-inch-long bugs. Within minutes of the start of the hatch, trout bulge to the surface to sip emergers and gulp duns. As the hatch proceeds, the emergence soon intensifies until the water is carpeted with duns and every trout is feeding greedily. Clumps of brown drakes float in groups and they are so thick that, after every three or four casts, your fly may need to be cleaned of the nymphal shucks that adhere to the fly's hackles. While fish become less selective as the deluge gets underway, fly placement and timing remain critical to fooling these trout.

The intensity of the action is apparent as soon as a fish is caught. As you attempt to remove your hook, the drakes dribble out of the trout's mouth. The brown drake hatch is as good a display of violence and death as found in any good action movie.

Morning spinner falls that follow the evening brown drake hatch are fairly common, but unpredictable. If you should come across this phenomenon, you are truly blessed. It is a fly fisherman's dream: big flies, big fish, big takes. And best of all, you can actually see what you're doing.

By the way, if you think you're going to be fishing all by yourself during the brown drake hatch – think again!

Priest Rapids

On lower Silver Creek, a small, one-mile portion of the stream is accessible to fishermen at a Bureau of Land Management site known as Priest Rapids. After leaving the meadow and foothill country so characteristic of upper Silver Creek, the personality of the stream rapidly changes as it suddenly runs over lava rocks and drops through a canyon of basalt. A short road provides access to the upper end of the canyon where fast-flowing Silver Creek creates ripples, pocket water, and shallow pools.

The road follows the creek along the rim of the canyon and then drops down to where Silver Creek exits the canyon and the flow slows and flattens. Past this point, the stream meanders through several cow pastures.

On this section of Silver Creek, mayflies have all but disappeared. They are by far outnumbered by good populations of caddis, stone, damsels, and dragonflies. Stoneflies – Pteronarcy californica – hatch in this area during March and April before the fishing season opens. Their nymphs are always good producers, however, in the faster stretches of water. The best hatches in this area are produced by several different species of caddis flies that usually appear in the evening. There are also plenty of grassy banks in this area that support a good grasshopper population and the best fishing of the season is often mid-day hopper fishing in late summer.

Priest Rapids is usually only an afterthought for local fishermen. Most anglers using this section spend the morning fishing the latest mayfly hatch on the Silver Creek Preserve and move down onto this section in the afternoon when the wind blows them off of the upper stream. The canyon at Priest Rapids serves as a wind break and allows you to fish on even the worst of days. Since few fishermen fish from dawn to dusk, Priest Rapids is often deserted by evening when the best caddis hatches occur.

This section of Silver Creek is a real sleeper. While fishing here, I have seen one huge brown trout after another stake out their territory as they stalk smaller fish. It's very common for the evening's calm to be abruptly interrupted by a brown trout rising to take a shiners which are feeding on bugs on the surface. The trout's vicious slamming of these three-inch fish resembles the same effect as throwing a concrete block into the water.

If you are there on enough evenings, you notice that all the activity in the evening is taking place at fifty-yard intervals along the stream. Apparently, when on the prowl, monster browns don't like to intermix with their heavyweight brethren. Big olive-brown and dirty-white, Woolhead Streamers are good imitations of the shiners the browns are hunting and I have had some tremendous strikes when fishing these flies just under the surface. When big browns are lined up at their feeding stations, hoppers, Wooly Buggers, and matukas are all potentially deadly offerings. Leaders should be cut back to at least 4X for this type of fishing and even this often doesn't prove to be strong enough.

My most memorable experience on this stretch of stream occurred on one of those cool September evenings when, not having seen another person in hours, it seemed I was the only person on earth. I was just going through the motions of stripping a Muddler Minnow from one side of the stream to the other, when a brown hit with a jolting strike.

As I started to work the twenty-inch fish towards the bank, I found myself wondering why I always managed to hook big fish when no one else was around to be impressed. But just then, an old, battered Ford pickup came down the road and into the BLM campsite where I was playing the fish. As the dust

Priest Rapids

cleared, a couple of cowboy-hatted teenagers jumped out to watch me take on the behemoth.

Their only comment was "Hey, good fish," but you could tell by their tone that they found my fight exciting. As I played the trout, they asked what I had taken it on. And when I told them I was using a streamer, I could tell by their reaction that using anything but a worm or minnow on a hook was foreign to them.

As the fish played out and rolled on its side, I felt kind of proud as I pulled the hook-jawed male brown to the bank in front of my onlookers. When close to the bank, I gently landed the fish by hand and pulled the fly out of its mouth with my forceps. Then I slowly returned the fish to the water where I released it. Behind me, I heard the two boys respond as one, "What the hell are you doing?"

Expecting a standing ovation for my accomplishment, their comment stunned me. I looked up into disbelieving faces and they groaned again, "Why did you let that fish go?"

I told them that I always returned my fish so that they could be caught again. This made sense to me, but I could see that they wouldn't have been anymore shocked than if I had stripped naked and danced on the bank after I landed the fish.

We stood there for a few more seconds. They sized me up as a crazed psychotic. I thought God must love red-necks – he made so many of them. No one said a word. They got back in their truck and left in a blaze of exhaust fumes. I gathered up my gear and headed home.

Little Wood River

What was once a beautiful river of pocket water, huge deep pools and deep cut channels now typifies what can happen to a stream when man feels he has a right to use every last drop of water for his own pursuits. During the Idaho drought of the late-1980s and early 1990s, the Little Wood River nearly stopped flowing. Upstream, the river was being completely diverted for watering crops. Downstream, only the flow entering from Silver Creek kept water in the river's channel.

Remarkably, the brown trout in this river seemed to have survived the low water, lukewarm temperatures, and over abundance of slimy alga. But the rainbow trout were hit hard during these extreme conditions.

In the first season immediately following the drought, a friend and I were able to catch a dozen robust and even "fat" brown trout on each visit to the stream. It was an ominous sign, however, that neither of us caught a single rainbow in a stream that was a 50/50 mix of these two species before the drought.

Surprisingly, today, three years out of the drought, things are looking very good for both the rainbow and the brown trout. Suddenly, the population of rainbows has jumped and we are again catching as many of these as browns. A seventeen-inch rainbow recently hooked just down from Preacher's Bridge, made a magnificent series of seven jumps each time clearing the water by at least two feet. It never ceases to amaze me how quickly nature recovers from every disaster.

On a cyclic basis – every few years or so – huge plagues of hoppers develop in southern Idaho. During these periods, fishing the Little Wood is at its best. Just how good the fishing can be is judged by how loud the farmers are screaming at the Bureau of Land Management to poison the hoppers that have taken up residence on the federal land that adjoins their fields.

The louder they yell, the better you know the hopper fishing will be.

I have seen hoppers so thick on the banks of the Little Wood that, as you walked the stream's edge, every step would put half-a-dozen of these insects into the air and one or two into the water. At the peak of the hopper cycle, smart, old brown trout would line up along the bank to pick off any hoppers that were unfortunate enough to tumble into the fast water. Being even smarter, however, I can remember walking along the stream locating fish after fish by watching the hoppers drift in the current.

After drifting my own Joe's Hopper to one of these waiting mouths, I found myself tied into one of those fat browns that is less than eighteen inches in length but still weigh nearly four pounds. As I brought the trout to the bank, I could see its age carved in its face. The brown's lower jaw was strangely disfigured as if it had chomped down on a brick. The trout's nose was a dark blackish-chocolate and covered with a cross hatch of deep scars. And with what must be a near fatal injury for a trout, one of its eyes was glossed over and had turned white. The fish was definitely over-the-hill, but when I poked the bulging pot belly of this ancient, one-eyed old-timer, I could tell he was still able to nail his share of hoppers. Certain fish make you feel extra special when you release them. For me, this brown was one of those.

With normal to above-normal snowfalls in this area during 1996 and 1997 it shouldn't be long until the stream regains its old character. Always in the shadow of the reputation of its parent river, Silver Creek, the Little Wood has always been a favorite of local fishermen who want a place to fish where they could walk a mile or so of river and never see another soul.

Silver Creek has built its reputation on the slow water and unbelievable hatches that characterize the stream's upper end. But if you're willing to take the time to explore this special river, you'll find every type of water and an unbelievable variety of fishing can be found along its length. For me, life is not a dream, it's a stream – Silver Creek.

* * *

Public access to Idaho Streams

Over its course, Silver Creek and its tributaries flow over very little public property. Most of these streams are on private property and to access any of them by land, you must have the property owner's consent or you will be trespassing.

Although privately owned, if you abide by their regulations and sign in daily at their log cabin visitor center, The Nature Conservancy allows access to the land it manages at the headwaters of Silver Creek. Nearby areas with public access include Loving Creek at Hayspur Hatchery, the sportsman's access managed by the Fish and Game Department at Point of Rocks, and an access on Bureau of Land Management land on lower

Silver Creek. All other land adjoining the stream is under private ownership and you need to get permission before entering it.

Just to insure you understand the law, the state of Idaho does provides for legal access to public waters that are considered navigable. Specifically, Idaho Fish and Game Title 36, Section 36-1601 states:

a) Navigable Streams Defined. Any stream which, in its natural state, during normal high water, will float cut timber having a diameter in excess of six (6) inches or any other commercial or floatable commodity or is capable of being navigated by oar or motor propelled small craft for pleasure or commercial purposes is navigable.

b) Recreational Use Authorized. Navigable rivers, sloughs or streams within the meander lines or, when not meandered, between the flow lines of ordinary high water thereof, and of all rivers, sloughs and streams flowing through any public lands of the state shall be open to public use as a public highway for travel and passage, up or downstream, for business or pleasure, and to exercise the incidents of navigation— boating, swimming, fishing, hunting and all recreational purposes.

c) Access Limited to Navigable Stream. Nothing herein contained shall authorize the entering on or crossing over private land at any point other than within the high water lines of navigable streams except that where irrigation dams or other obstructions interfere with the navigability of a steam, members of the public may remove themselves from their boats, floats, canoes or other floating crafts from the stream and walk or portage such crafts around said obstruction re-entering the stream immediately below such obstruction at the nearest point where it is safe to do so.

If all of this legalese seems a bit antiquated, confusing, and inconclusive then you probably understand it as well as anyone. For now, depending on who you talk to, you will get differing opinions on which streams qualify for public access under this regulation. To date, only Silver Creek itself has been legally declared to be a navigable, public highway. In the future, the courts may have to settle the question of the status of its tributaries.

Fishing Seasons and Regulations

Season: Upstream from Highway 93, Silver Creek and its tributaries are open for fishing from the Saturday of Memorial Day Weekend through November 30. Downstream from Highway 93, Silver Creek is open all year.

Special Regulations and Restrictions:

From Highway 93 upstream to the county road bridge north of Picabo – General Rules apply

From the county road bridge north of Picabo upstream to the bridge at milepost 187.2 on Highway 20 west of Picabo – two trout may be taken – none between 12"-16"

From the bridge at milepost 187.2 on U.S. Highway 20 west of Picabo upstream to the road right-of-way fence on the west side of Kilpatrick Bridge – Catch-and-release – No fishing from rafts or boats. Float tubes permissible.

From the road right-of-way fence on the west side of Kilpatrick Bridge upstream and all waters within The Nature Conservancy Silver Creek Preserve property – Fly Fishing only – Catch-and-release – No fishing from rafts or boats – Float tubes permissible.

Because regulations are subject to change, you are encouraged to obtain a copy of the current Idaho General Fishing Seasons and Rules.

This publication and other information can be obtained from:

Idaho Department of Fish and Game, Magic Valley Region
868 E. Main St.,
P.O. Box 428
Jerome, ID 83338
(208) 324-4359

Information about fishing the Silver Creek Preserve can be obtained from:
Silver Creek Preserve
P.O. Box 624
Picabo, ID 83348
(208)-788-2203

9
Even More

Fishing Silver Creek provides enough excitement for an entire vacation or a summer season, but even the most dedicated of fly fishermen occasionally like to lay their rod down and try something a little different.

Bird Watching

There are not many better places in Idaho for watching waterfowl, seeing raptors, and listening to song birds than the Silver Creek Preserve. In mid- May, which may be the best time to catch both resident and migrating birds at the stream, an early morning visit is like going to a zoo aviary – a very noisy aviary.

In the spring, from one end of the Silver Creek Preserve to the other, you hear dozens of Canada geese honk and cackle as they sort out who is going to do the breeding this year. In nearby farm fields, ring-billed gulls squawk as they dine on a

Sandhill cranes

banquet of insects tilled up by tractors used by farmers for planting. And seemingly from the tattered top of every one of last year's cattail spikes, a red-winged blackbird calls its mate. For the dedicated birder, Silver Creek is a great place to spot most of the birds commonly found in Idaho. On a recent sunny day in May, another birder and I were able to identify more than fifty different species of birds within just a few hours.

Of interest to the bird watcher looking for a few out- of-the-ordinary birds, this same hike turned up a willet, a long-billed dowitcher, a pair of Caspian terns, a canvasback, and several groups of sandhill cranes. Raptors were also plentiful; we spotted one sharp-shinned hawk, one Cooper's hawk, one prairie falcon, numerous red-tailed hawks, northern harriers, and American kestrels.

I find it a challenge to locate and identify many different species of birds while hiking in the Preserve, but I find that watching the drama that takes place in the day-to-day life of the birds even more exciting. At Silver Creek, I have watched the blue herons stalk small fish in the shallows and then stab them with their long bills. I have seen a kingfisher hover ten feet over the water and then, by rapidly folding both wings, drop like a rock into the water only to reappear a few seconds later, carrying a three-inch minnow in its beak. And then there was that time, I came upon a cinnamon teal resting on a small puddle of water in the middle of an aspen grove. Suddenly, the duck became visibly nervous and lifted off of the water in a complete panic. I thought the duck was reacting to my presence until, an instant later, a Cooper's hawk flashed into the opening and headed for the flapping, squawking teal. As the duck rose, it smacked a wing on a branch and began to tumble. Seeing its opportunity, the hawk dropped its claws and attacked. Fortunately for the duck, the hawk hit the same jutting branch and missed its target. Last seen, both birds were headed into the thick stand of trees at breakneck speed.

Canoeing

We don't do much of anything slowly anymore. That's why canoeing, done at a speed of less than one-mile-per-hour, is such a remarkably different experience. In a way, it's like meditating – you become absorbed by the gentle motion of the water, the faint calls of songbirds and the swirling breezes until the rest of the world and all of its problems just fade away.

The most popular area to canoe on Silver Creek is the slow waters of the Preserve. Good places to launch a canoe are limited, but an ideal put in site is located at the bridge where one of the main gravel road into the Preserve crosses the headwaters of Stalker Creek. For about one mile below this bridge, the stream is quite shallow and, early in the summer, gravel bars may only be covered by a few inches of water. Using a canoe with a shallow draft and limiting the load and number of people you carry will help when it comes to crossing these shallow areas. But even if you do high center, by getting out and dragging your canoe a few yards, you can quickly get to deeper water. Later in the summer, an increase in flow from the feeder springs and a burst of growth by aquatic plants both cause the water level to rise and eliminate shallow- water problems.

After floating the three miles through the Preserve, you come to a natural takeout site at Kilpatrick Bridge. If you have left your vehicle here or, if you are one of those enjoy a day filled with activity and have left a mountain bike at the bridge, you can quickly drive or pedal two miles back to your vehicle at Stalker Creek.

While canoeing on Silver Creek, it is always best to interfere as little as possible with fishermen. Most anglers will show you the water they don't want you to float through by casting in that direction. As a fisherman, I find I am at first irritated when canoers violate "my" space. I find, however, that if the paddlers say "howdy" and ask how the fishing is, I welcome their intrusion.

Serious fishermen should try canoeing Silver Creek for two reasons. First, this is the best way to get a feeling of just how complex this elongated ecosystem is. While traveling down stream, it becomes readily apparent that fish are not evenly distributed, but have preferred locations and water types where they tend to concentrate. These select areas may change slightly during different periods of the year, but it is helpful to locate key areas inhabited by good fish.

The variety and density of different insects hatches on Silver Creek is also something that can best be appreciated while moving from point to point. By floating the stream, you can see that some hatches occur along the entire length of the stream while other emergences are restricted to specific types of water. It also becomes apparent that some hatches are found in areas as small as a single bend in the stream. When all of this is put into your fly fishing computer, you get a much better sense of the complexity of the Silver Creek ecosystem.

Camping

Few campgrounds are exciting enough to be considered an activity in themselves, but the Hayspur campground is one of those wonderful exceptions. The only campground in the immediate vicinity of Silver Creek, the parklike grounds are a portion of the Hayspur Hatchery managed by the Idaho Fish and Game Department. Here, you don't have to camp on one of those little slots of asphalt provided at most recreational campgrounds, you simply select your space under one of the several trees scattered about on a large, grassy (but mown) meadow.

As you might expect with this much freedom, you must be content with rather limited services. There is no water at the campground and only the most basic of privies, but when is the last time you heard this–there is no fee for camping here!

What makes Hayspur different than most campsites is the adjacent hatchery operation. Almost every rainbow trout stocked into the put-and-take waters of Idaho begins life in the concrete runs of Hayspur. Some of the fish are raised to a catchable size of ten inches but most are whisked away to other hatcheries throughout the state when still eggs. In recent years, the Fish and Game Departmenthas been producing – with a little help from the fish–nearly twelve million trout eggs annually at Hayspur.

An attraction right on site is Gaver Lagoon. This small pond is stocked with 500 to 1,000 fish every week during the summer and is a perfect place for younger fly fisherman to catch their first fish. Since excess brood fish of up to seven pounds are dumped into Gaver Lagoon every spring and fall, there is also the chance that mom and dad may want to try a few casts themselves. In accordance with Idaho's fish and game regulations, a general limit of fish may be taken at the lagoon and there is no restriction on the type of gear used. Bait, lures and flies are all allowed here.

Photography

The biggest problem a photographer has at Silver Creek is deciding what subject to capture on film. Spectacular images are everywhere. Silver Creek landscapes are like no other in world. Seldom as photogenic in the morning or in the bright sunlight of day, Silver Creek is best photographed in the evening. The colors are fantastic – reds, yellows, greens and purples – all under a blue sky occasionally made even more dramatic by billowing cumulus clouds rising high over the Pioneer and Sawtooth Mountains. But it's not the color that sets Silver Creek apart, it's the glow.

It's hard to describe the play of color that takes place at Silver Creek late in the day. As the sun begins to set, the entire landscape is bathed in a radiant, warm, remarkably pleasant light. The unique blend of earthy colors is caused by a combination of low light playing off pale sage and grass covered hills, deep green willows, that is set of by, yes, the silver sparkle of Silver Creek.

For the photographer, there are four distinct seasons at Silver Creek. Spring, when everything is fresh and new-green. Summer, a time of thunder storms and bright days. Fall, when a dry dust produces a haze in the air and the orange, yellow and red of the aspen and willow leaves produce an autumn blaze. And Winter, when rime ice coats the bushes, steam rises from the water, and blizzards sculpt and carve the snow. To truly capture the essence of this stream, you must photograph all of its faces.

If you carry a pocket camera, it's possible to take a quick photo of any fish caught. Instead of pitching the trout up on the bank in order to get your fly rod in for scale, try leaving the fish in your net and keeping it in the water. Better yet, get your friend to take a photo of you cradling the fish in your hands. For the trout's benefit, make sure it is returned to the stream as soon as possible.

And while taking pictures of fish is something we all do, do yourself and any potential viewers a favor by taking a few photos of the background as well. Photos of friends fishing, closeups of flies used, full-blown hatches that flicker in the low evening sun, and the different types of water found at Silver Creek all make a much more interesting album or program for the local trout club than an endless string of me-and-my-fish photos.

For those interested in wildlife photography, Silver Creek offers wonderful opportunities. Mule deer can frequently be photographed at dawn or dusk as they roam the farm fields and meadows of the area. Since these animals are protected from hunting within The Nature Conservancy, they are generally easy to approach. While walking along the bank during a recent fishing trip, I nearly stumbled over a small, three-point buck bedded beneath a willow. The deer watched me at a distance of three feet for a good minute before it finally took off and I continued on my way.

Later, as I returned along this same path, I was surprised to find that the deer was back into its bed and was again reluctant to leave even when I was only inches away. I've hunted mule deer all of my life and this is the first time I have seen an animal that was so accustomed to people that it would feel safe in the same bed it had been spooked from just hours before. Birds and other animals are also abundant and you won't have to compete with other photographers like in the more popular wildlife viewing areas such as Yellowstone National Park.

Hiking

If you're looking for something to do between hatches, are a bored, non-fishing spouse, or if you just want to get to know the high desert better, there are a couple of hikes at Silver Creek you should consider taking. If you don't wear waders – and I doubt you do your best hiking while covered from armpits-to-toes in neoprene–you must be sure to pick a route that allows you to cross at one of the several bridges that span the stream.

Within The Nature Conservancy's property, your best bet for a long hike is to leave from the visitor center and walk upstream until you come to the wooden boardwalk at the outlet creek of Sullivan Lake. After crossing, you walk past a large stand of aspen groves until reaching an old bridge that allows you to cross to the north side of the stream. Once on the other side, you have a choice of following the stream or cutting across a couple of fallow-at least for now–farm fields. Either way, you eventually come to Loving Creek, where you head upstream for about one-fourth mile until you find the bridge that crosses this stream. From here, it is an easy walk to Kilpatrick Bridge located on the main road into the preserve.

From Kilpatrick Bridge, you can then wander along the southern banks of Silver Creek or follow the road back to the visitor center. Depending on which path you chose, the circular route covers between three and four miles. With no true trail to follow, this hike takes several hours to complete.

Self-guided Nature Trail

The nature trail that starts at The Nature Conservancy cabin provides an opportunity to quickly orientate yourself to the high desert/riparian ecosystem represented at Silver Creek. The one-mile trail will introduce you to the sagebrush, riparian, wetland, and stream habitats and plants that make up this environment. A trail guide for use along this path can be obtained at the vistor center.

In less than one hour, this trail will show you where Silver Creek is born, identify the most common native plants of the area, and provide an opportunity to see a few of stream's most famous residents–the trout. For an even more enjoyable experience carry a pair of binoculars and a set of bird and plant identification books. Taking along a little mosquito repellant is also a good idea.

Cross-country Skiing

With a host of nearby places to ski – Sun Valley, Soldier Mountain, Stanley Basin – few skiers take advantage of Silver Creek in the winter. Although you'll often have to break your own trail, the solitude provided at Silver Creek more than makes up for the extra effort. It's a good idea to come with a friend so you can switch off with the job of breaking trail through the twelve to twenty-four inches of snowpack that accumulates by late winter.

Cross-country skiers often get a close look
at the wildlife that winter at Silver Creek.

A few hours of skiing along the flats that border Silver
Creek offers a chance to see hundreds of different waterfowl.
Most of the ducks will be green-headed mallards, but nearly
every species of waterfowl that winter in Idaho can be found
soaking in the "warm" water of Silver Creek. Waterfowl found
here include the sculptured white, gray, and black pintail usually seen feeding with its pointed butt pointed into the air, gold-
eneyes that have a distinctive white dot the size of a nickel tat-
tooed on their cheeks, and American widgeons, the duck that
wears a white stripe on the top of its head, and at least a half-
dozen other ducks and geese.

Away from the water, tracks and trails in the snow are good
indicators that many other animals spend the winter near
Silver Creek. Under the willows you see dozens of four-inch
wide trails that form unruly mazes beneath the vegetation. On
sunny days, you see the creature that created this labyrinth of
animal highways—the cottontail rabbit. It's easier for you to recognize that the much larger trails that weave through these
same willow patches were left by some of the estimated 100
mule deer that spend the winter here, away from the deep snow
drifts of the surrounding mountains. And when you come across

the mosaics of webbed footprints that cover the snow along the stream, you immediately know your have identified the locations where Canadian geese like to strut.

When you come to a small pile of feathers and a few sprinkles of red on an otherwise undisturbed patch of pure white snow, there is a sense of having discovered a small mystery. Turning amateur detective, you examine the feathers and find them to be those of a duck–probably a gadwall. When this information is coupled with your recollection of a red-tailed hawk you saw perched in one of the barren branches of a nearby aspen, you feel comfortable in convicting the bird on circumstantial evidence; the scene in front of you is nothing more than a redtail hawk feast.

Other Nearby Attractions

Within an easy drive of Silver Creek are several other attractions that offer some solace if winds are blowing too strongly on the stream. The Sawtooth National Recreation Area is managed by the US Forest Service and is located just north of Ketchum. In most states, the White Cloud and Sawtooth Mountain ranges would be enshrined as national parks, but in Idaho, these sculpted spires are just a couple of more mountain ranges and remain unknown to all but local residents. Truly as spectacular as the Grand Tetons and parts of the Rocky Mountains, the valleys between these highlands offer other opportunities for camping, fishing, or boating on some of the numerous lakes in this area. Hiking trails are scattered throughout the forest and information on specific routes can be obtained at the Forest Service visitor center eight miles north of Ketchum.

A half-hour ride east of Silver Creek is Craters of the Moon National Monument. This National Park area offers an experience seemingly designed to be the opposite of that offered in the adjacent Pioneer Mountains. Here a barren, bleak landscape of cinders and lava greet you. This site, under the auspices of the National Park Service, offers plenty of opportunities to explore a terrain that seems from another world. Trails lead to the top of small volcanoes, over rugged oceans of black lava rock, and below the surface where lava drained from beneath the lava flows leaving hollow tubes or caves behind.

And if you haven't yet had your fill of fishing Silver Creek, there are a great many other streams where you may want to wet your line. The Big Wood River in the Ketchum area, the South Fork of the Boise River to the west, and the Big Lost River on the other side of the mountains near Mackay and Arco offer good to great freestone river fishing.

One of the most spectacular auto tours that can be taken in the United States is a circular route that leaves from Silver Creek, heads up over Galena Summit, and follows the Salmon River. The road winds along the river until you reach Challis and then proceeds south between two mountain ranges. At Arco, you turn west again and head through Carey, and arrive once again at Picabo and Silver Creek.

Along the way, you can catch a glimpse of the home of the late Ernest Hemingway (have a local point it out to you – it's not open to visitors), stop at the Idaho State Fish Hatchery where they're trying to save the last of Idaho's salmon runs, and walk on the sandy beach that borders the aquamarine waters of Red Fish Lake. Or you can stop and throw a cast or two for steelhead in the Salmon River, see a historic gold mining operation at Yankee Fork, or visit the black rock terrain at Craters of the Moon National Monument. A mixed bag along a route approximately 300 miles in length that can be done in a day, but deserves more.

Although it may be the trout of Silver Creek that bring you to the state, make sure you don't miss any of the other incredible sights or adventures that are found everywhere in central Idaho. And when you tackle Silver Creek, give yourself a chance to enjoy it. Relax and remember why it is you fly fish. For us it is best stated in those famous words of Robert Traver in *Trout Magic*, "I fish . . . not because I regard fishing as being so terribly important but because I suspect that so many other concerns of men are equally unimportant – and not nearly so much fun."

Truly words to live by.

The Authors

David Glasscock

David has been pursuing trout and guiding fly fishermen on Silver Creek and surrounding rivers since 1980. He is licensed with the state of Idaho as an outfitter and guide and owns and operates Idaho Angling Services. David and his wife, Ginny, live in the small ranching community of Picabo, in the Silver Creek Valley. Living only minutes from the banks of Silver Creek affords David the chance to flyfish most every day of the summer and fall.

Since 1986, David has been spending the winters living in New Zealand. He is based on the South Island, traveling to both islands to fish the multitude of waters the country has to offer. David organizes and plans itineraries for anglers visiting New Zealand.

Idaho Angling Services L.L.C.
P.O. Box 703, Picabo, ID 83348
Phone 208-788-9709
Web Site http://home.rmci.net/anglingservices/

David Clark

Dave fished Silver Creek for the first time in 1978 and still remembers that first, tough rainbow he caught on an elk hair caddis. Nearly twenty years later, he considers this stream his "home water."

Dave also is a freelance writer who has had articles on Silver Creek published in *Fly Fisherman, Fly Fishing, Fins and Feathers* and *Oh! Idaho*. His articles have appeared in *Western Horseman, Parks and Wildlife, Rocky Mountain Fish and Game* and several other regional magazines. Dave wrote and photographed *Unearthly Landscape,* published by the Craters of the Moon Natural History Association in 1992, served as science editor and writer/photographer for *Snake: The Plain and its People*, Published in 1994 by Boise State University.

Rt. 1, Box 312, Arco, ID 83213

Appendix

Basic Silver Creek Fly Patterns

DRY FLIES

Pale Morning Dun (Ephemerella)
Size: 14 -20
Body Color: Yellow/Olive
Wings: Pale-gray/Yellowish or Clear
Tails: Three

Suggested fly patterns:

*Poly Parachute
*Poly-wing Spinner
*Compara-dun
*Light Cahill
*No-hackle
*Sparkle-dun
*Yellow Humpy
*Parachute Adams

Brown Drake (Ephemera)
Size: 10-12
Body Color: Yellowish-tan/Brown
Wing Color: Dun/Speckled or Clear/Speckled
Tails: Three

Green Drake (Drunella)
Size: 10-12
Body Color: Green
Wing Color: Dun/Speckled
Tails: 3

Gray Drake (Siphlonurus)
Size: 10-12
Body Color: Gray
Wing Color: Dun/Speckled
Tails: 3

Suggested fly patterns:

*Poly Parachute
*Poly-wing Spinner
*Extended Body Parachute
*Extended Body Spinner
*Parachute Cripple
*Quigley Cripple

Blue-winged Olive (Baetis)
Size: 18-24
Body Color: Light to Dark Olive
Wing Color: Slate-gray or Clear
Tails: Two

Suggested fly patterns:

*Poly Parachute
*Poly-wing Spinner
*No-Hackle
*Cripple Biot Dun
*Griffith's Gnat
*CDC BWO
*Parachute Adams
*Adams

Tricos (Tricorythodes)
Size: 18-24
Body Color: Black or Olive
Wings: Whitish-gray or Clear
Tails: Three

Suggested fly patterns:

*Poly-wing Spinner
*No-hackle
*Biot Body Spinner
*CDC Trico
*Double Poly-wing Spinner

Speckled Dun (Callibaetis)
Size: 14-18
Body Color: Light to Dark Grayish
or Tan/Brown
Wing: Speckled Grey/Brown or
Speckled/Clear
Tails: Two

Suggested fly patterns:

*Poly Parachute
*Poly-wing Spinner
*Adams
*Parachute Adams
*Quigley Cripple
*Partridge-wing Spinner

**Mahogany Dun
(Paraleptophlebia)**
Size: 14-16
Body Color: Reddish-Brown
Wing: Slate-gray or Clear
Tails:Three

Suggested fly patterns:

*Poly Parachute
*Poly-wing Spinner
*Quigley Cripple
*No-hackle
*Quill Gordon

Caddis
Size: 10-22

Suggested fly patterns:

*Elk Hair Caddis
*Henryville
*Slow Water Caddis
*Delta-wing Caddis
*Parachute Caddis

Midges
Size: 18-24

Suggested fly patterns:

*Griffith's Gnat
*Winged Black Midge

Stoneflies
Size: 14-16

Suggested fly patterns:

*Stimulator
*Yellow Sally

Damselflies
Size: 12-16

Suggested fly patterns:

*Extended Body Parachute
*Braided-Butt Damsel

Terrestials

Suggested fly patterns:

*Crowe's Beetle
*High Visibility Beetle
*Flying Ant
*Deer Hair Ant
*Fur Ant
*Dave's Hopper
*Joe's Hopper
*Parachute Hopper

NYMPHS/PUPA/LARVA

Mayflies –

Suggested fly patterns:

*Pheasant Tail
*Pheasant Tail Bead Head
*Gold Ribbed Hare's Ear
*Gold Ribbed Hare's Ear Bead Head
*Hare's Ear Parachute
*Gray Muskrat
*AP Nymphs
*Floating Nymphs
*CDC Emergers

Caddis –

Suggested fly patterns:

*Sparkle
*Soft Hackle
*Peeking

Midge –

Suggested fly patterns:

*Palomino Midge
*Serendipity
*Suspender
*Brassie

Damselflies –

Suggested fly patterns:

Marabou Damsel

Scuds –

Suggested fly patterns:

*Olive/tan Scud

Minnows/Chubs

Suggested fly patterns:

*Woolhead Sculpin
*Mituka
*Muddler Minnow

Leeches

Suggested fly patterns:

*Wooly Bugger
*Marabou Leech

Index

Other Caxton Books About Idaho

River Tales of Idaho
by Darcy Williamson
ISBN 0-87004-378-1 342 pages paper $17.95

The Cabin on Sawmill Creek
A Western Walden
by Mary Jo Churchwell
ISBN 0-87004-380-3 240 pages paper $12.95

Southern Idaho Ghost Towns
by Wayne Sparling
ISBN 0-87004-229-7 135 pages paper $12.95

Gem Minerals of Idaho
by John A. Beckwith
ISBN 0-87004-228-9 129 pages paper $9.95

Tiger on the Road
The Life of Vardis Fisher
by Tim Woodword
ISBN 0-87004-333-1 269 pages paper $14.95
ISBN 0-87004-338-2 cloth $19.95

For a free catalog of Caxton books write to:

The CAXTON PRINTERS, Ltd.
Publishing Department
312 Main Street
Caldwell, ID 83605

or

Visit our Internet Website:

www.caxtonprinters.com

WC